Journaling

by Amber Lea Starfire, MFA

Journaling For Dummies®

Published by: **John Wiley & Sons, Inc.**, 111 River Street, Hoboken, NJ 07030-5774,
www.wiley.com

Copyright © 2023 by John Wiley & Sons, Inc., Hoboken, New Jersey

Published simultaneously in Canada

For general information on our other products and services, please contact our Customer Care Department within the U.S. at 877-762-2974, outside the U.S. at 317-572-3993, or fax 317-572-4002. For technical support, please visit www.wiley.com/techsupport.

Wiley publishes in a variety of print and electronic formats and by print-on-demand. Some material included with standard print versions of this book may not be included in e-books or in print-on-demand. If this book refers to media such as a CD or DVD that is not included in the version you purchased, you may download this material at http://booksupport.wiley.com. For more information about Wiley products, visit www.wiley.com.

Library of Congress Control Number is available from the publisher.

ISBN 978-1-119-90041-2 (pbk); ISBN 978-1-119-90042-9 (ebk);
ISBN 978-1-119-90043-6 (ebk)

SKY10035957_091222

Table of Contents

PART 2: EXPLORING POPULAR JOURNALING TECHNIQUES 71

Introduction

You've heard it said that life is a journey — amazingly beautiful at times, and yet also complicated and messy. Along this journey, you experience myriad emotions, ranging from despair to joy, and have to deal with countless decision points, from trivial to life-changing. No one is exempt from life's challenges, and everyone needs help navigating the confusing events, responses, relationships, and choices that are simply part of being human.

Fortunately, journaling is a simple and effective tool that helps you address all of life's issues. Moreover, it's inexpensive and freely available to everyone — and that includes you.

This book can show you what you need to begin and maintain a journal, as well as how to use your journal to improve your life. The techniques and guidance provided in these pages can help you process and make meaning of significant life events, enhance self-awareness, identify ineffective or harmful habits and behaviors, build gratitude, establish a positive outlook on life, become better organized, solve difficult problems, and achieve your most important goals. That list of results may seem like a lot to promise, yet journaling has helped tens of thousands of people achieve these positive outcomes.

In these pages, you can discover how to practice journaling in ways that work best for you, so that you can continue to be engaged and maintain your journaling routines for years to come. While you grow in your knowledge and expand your journaling methods, you can expect to reap many of its benefits, ultimately attaining a greater sense of well-being and purpose.

About This Book

I wrote *Journaling For Dummies* with both beginners and experienced journal writers in mind.

If you're a beginner, this book provides you with all the information that you need to figure out if and how journaling can work for you, how to get started, and the tools you need.

If you've journaled before and want to reignite or deepen your practice, *Journaling For Dummies* provides a rich resource that offers a variety of journaling techniques, prompts, and inspirational ideas.

To make the information accessible, I've divided the book into four parts:

>> **Part 1: Getting Started with Journaling:** Foundational information that you need to understand what journaling can do for you, how to get started, and how to fit it into your life.

>> **Part 2: Exploring Popular Journaling Techniques:** Takes a deep dive into five different methods — reflective, mindful, Bullet, creative, and gratitude journaling.

>> **Part 3: Journaling Your Way to Health and Happiness:** Shows you how to apply the different methods for specific purposes, including healing emotional trauma, improving relationships, becoming more creative, achieving your goals, exploring your spirituality, and journeying through grief.

>> **Part 4: The Part of Tens:** Offers tips to maintain a robust journaling practice and ways to generate your own journaling prompts.

Whatever your knowledge and experience level, you can find what you need in *Journaling For Dummies* to begin and develop your journaling practice. Feel free to work your way through the content in any order you choose — skip around according to your interest, or start at the beginning and work your way through all the techniques and topics.

Foolish Assumptions

In writing this book, I made a few assumptions about who you are and why you opened these pages:

>> You've either heard about journaling or tried it before, and you think it could help you. Or you already journal on a regular basis and are looking for ways to deepen your practice.

>> You're interested in discovering more about yourself, your inner workings, and why you respond the way you do in relationships and life events.

>> You might feel a little shy or intimidated about expressing your inner feelings and thoughts — or maybe you've unsuccessfully tried journaling in the past — and you're looking for guidance on ways to get started and maintain a fulfilling practice.

>> You want to have more clarity and improve the quality of your decisions.

>> You want to improve your mental, emotional, and physical health and your relationships.

Icons Used in This Book

Throughout this book, icons in the margins highlight certain types of valuable information that call for your attention. Here are the icons you encounter and a brief description of each.

TIP

The Tip icon marks information that can help you make decisions about how you want to approach certain topics or prompts more easily; they might also provide inspirational variations of prompts.

REMEMBER

Remember icons mark information that's especially important to know. To identify the most important information in each chapter, just skim through these icons.

WARNING

The Warning icon tells you to be careful. It marks important information that can help you navigate difficult journaling topics and issues in safe ways.

Beyond the Book

In addition to the abundance of information and guidance related to journaling that I provide in this book, you get access to even more help and information online at Dummies.com. Check out this book's online Cheat Sheet. Just go to www.dummies.com and search for *Journaling For Dummies Cheat Sheet*.

Where to Go from Here

Although you don't need to go through *Journaling For Dummies* in any particular order, for best results, ask yourself, "What am I looking to gain by journaling?" The answer to this question can guide you to the chapters and topics that best meet your needs.

That said, I do have a few recommendations about how to approach the content in this book:

>> For beginners:

- If you've never journaled before, I highly recommend going through Part 1 first. Then, select a method in Part 2 that appeals to you and give it a try.

- If you want to know more about journaling's benefits, be sure to go through Chapter 2.

- If you have concerns or fears about journaling, see Chapter 4 for how to overcome your fear.

>> If you've attempted journaling before and had difficulty making it a regular part of your life, I suggest looking at Chapter 3 and Chapter 4 before diving into specific journaling methods or topics.

» For experienced journal writers:

- If you're looking to expand or deepen your journaling, I recommend trying a new method. Check out the different ways to journal in Part 2. Then, challenge yourself to begin something completely different.

  For example, if you've only used the written word to journal, try creative journaling, which incorporates drawing and other visual journaling methods (see Chapter 8).

- You may also find a topic in Part 3 that can inspire you to new insights.

1
Getting Started with Journaling

Discover what journaling can do for you, what you need to get started, and how to integrate a journaling practice into your life.

Examine the many benefits of journaling and how to overcome any obstacles that might prevent you from journaling successfully.

Create a foundation for an enduring practice by identifying your motivations, deciding how you want to journal, gathering your tools, and setting up your writing space.

Take the steps you need to establish your journaling practice.

Chapter 1

Exploring Life with Journaling

Discovering the world of journal writing — also known as journaling — is to find, all at once, unlimited and creative personal expression; a way of exploring, investigating, and making meaning of life; and a self-help tool for increased self-knowledge and confidence.

With a regular journal-writing practice, you can create a safe space in which to express your deepest fears and hopes, disappointments and satisfactions, heartaches and joys. By writing down your feelings, thoughts, attitudes, and beliefs, you can discover behavioral patterns, become more self-aware, and improve your ability to learn from and build on significant life events.

Exploring the variety of journal-writing approaches in this book can help you find the methods that work best for you and provide you with the most meaningful benefits. And you can develop and deepen your journaling experience by practicing it on a regular basis, on a schedule and duration that fits your unique lifestyle.

In this chapter, I provide an overview of what journaling is and isn't as well as some of the different ways to approach journaling to help determine which journaling practice is a good fit for you and your lifestyle.

Defining Journaling

Journaling is the deeply personal practice of writing for personal development. It uses a variety of methods for recording life events, processing thoughts and emotions, increasing self-awareness and understanding, and achieving success through improved organization systems.

Journaling is similar to the once-commonplace practice of keeping a *diary* — a simple record of daily events. But with journaling, you take a deeper look at your life experience.

Whether you're brand new to journaling or have journaled in the past, you may have a few preconceptions about journal writing that could limit your approach to it. When you think about beginning or resuming a journaling practice, understanding what journaling is and isn't can help you approach journaling with a willingness to experiment and find a method that works best for you.

Appreciating what journaling is

At its essence, journaling is a self-help tool that is

» Open-ended and flexible

» Personal and private (not designed for publication)

» A place to freely express feelings and thoughts, and to explore any topic of interest

» Designed to fit your lifestyle and schedule

» Relaxing and enjoyable

» Beneficial for mental, emotional, and physical health

» Used alone or in combination with professional psychological/mental health counseling and other services

Recognizing what journaling isn't

Because journaling can be adapted in unique ways for each person, it's not a one-size-fits-all form of exploring life's meaning and experiences. Here are a few other things that journaling is *not* meant to be or do.

>> Not a substitute for professional psychological or mental health services if you want or need help that a professional can provide.

>> Not rule-based or rigid.

>> Not focused on writing craft such as grammar, spelling, punctuation — or even full sentences. As long as you understand what you write, that's all that matters.

>> Not limited to writing — it may also include drawing, doodling, and other visual art forms.

Taking First Steps Toward Journaling Success

You may be wondering if journaling can work for you, and you probably have a few of the following questions: Will I enjoy writing? Will I be able to fit it into my schedule? Will it help me deal with some of the situations I'm experiencing?

Let me assure you that journaling is so flexible and effective that it works for just about everyone. The key to success is finding a method (or methods) and schedule that fit your lifestyle and feels comfortable.

TIP

To decide whether journaling is a good fit for you, it helps to understand your preferred communication style and your underlying reasons for considering journaling.

Determining your preferred communication style

Are you the sort of person who likes to talk out your problems with a close friend or confidante? Do you prefer reading and writing to watching videos? Do you enjoy working with your hands, perhaps with arts and crafts, or creating collages or scrapbooks? Do you practice or have you explored other self-help practices, such as mindfulness? Do you seek to better understand yourself?

If you answered yes to at least one of these questions, you likely can find journaling a natural extension of the ways in which you like to communicate and express yourself.

If you answered no to all of the questions, then journaling might not come naturally to you. That doesn't mean it's not for you, but you might have to work a little harder to find a method that feels natural and comfortable. If journaling doesn't come naturally, I recommend reviewing the different methods presented in this book and trying those that appeal to you.

Understanding your motivations

Why do you want to journal?

Although journaling has many benefits, what do you personally hope to gain from it? Answering this question and understanding what's drawing you to the idea of journaling can help you feel confident about your reasons for beginning or resuming a journaling practice.

For example, if you're interested in journaling because you want a safe place to express your most personal and private thoughts and feelings, that's a clear indication that journaling can benefit you.

On the other hand, if you're interested in journaling solely because someone told you that you *should* journal, then your motivation is externally based and may not be strong enough to carry you through the learning curve. In this case, answer the question: Why do *you* want to journal?

YOU'RE IN GOOD COMPANY: FAMOUS JOURNAL WRITERS

The practice of keeping a diary or journal is as ancient as writing itself. Some of the oldest discovered travel journals and writing that contain personal experience and inner reflections were created as early as 900 CE.

Here's a list of a few history-making journal keepers you might recognize:

- Meriwether Lewis, explorer (of Lewis and Clark)
- John Adams, second president of the United States
- Wolfgang Amadeus Mozart, composer
- Charles Darwin, naturalist
- Charlotte Brontë, novelist
- Henry David Thoreau, writer
- Vincent Van Gogh, artist
- Beatrix Potter, writer and illustrator
- Marie Curie, physicist and chemist
- Virginia Woolf, writer
- Carl Jung, psychiatrist and psychotherapist
- Anne Frank, diarist
- Frida Kahlo, artist

Still not sure? Browse the chapter titles and subjects in this book's Table of Contents, noting which ones appeal most to you or draw you in. That point of reference should help define what you're looking for in a journaling practice.

Introducing the Many Ways You Can Journal

Because journaling is unique to each person, there's no one right way to keep a journal. That said, there are some commonly used techniques and some techniques that have specific purposes or benefits. The chapters in Part 2 focus on particular methods, and the chapters in Part 3 focus on the reasons and benefits of journaling.

Writing without structure

The most common way to journal is to simply open your notebook (or digital app) and write or draw whatever is in your mind, whenever and for as long as you need. There's no specific format for filling a page. This way of journaling is often referred to as *free-writing.*

Free-writing (unstructured journaling) allows you to be in the moment with your thoughts and feelings, and to take a stream-of-consciousness approach to your journal.

Unstructured journal entries — and, in fact, entire journals — tend to meander across numerous time periods, topics, and situations. They can include prose, poems, sketches, doodles, and lists.

One drawback to unstructured journaling is that it can get boring after a while, especially if you tend to circle around the same topics over and over without gaining self-knowledge or increased understanding in the process. In this case, try another journaling method for a while (you can choose from the options in Part 2), just to mix things up.

Using writing prompts

The second most common way to journal, after free-writing (see the preceding section), is to use writing prompts. Prompts are helpful when you're not sure what you want to write about. And when you're feeling uninspired, a prompt can help engage the mind and start the creative juices flowing.

I'm a big proponent of journaling prompts, and I provide a lot of them throughout this book. I recommend journaling prompts to help you jumpstart your writing, approach a sensitive topic in new ways, get out of a journaling rut, and break through fear or writing blocks. Prompts can also help you deepen your journaling practice and gain meaningful insights.

REMEMBER

For best results, use prompts that interest you or generate an emotional response. You're not likely to write authentically or deeply in response to a journaling prompt that you're not engaged with.

Making lists and other structured forms

Lists and other highly structured forms of journaling, such as the Bullet Journal method (see Chapter 7), appeal to busy people who don't want to spend a lot of time writing but still want a way to document important events, keep track of tasks, and use shorthand to record emotional responses and thoughts.

Using a list structure is easy and fast, and it doesn't typically take a lot of mental or emotional energy. And it can still provide many of the benefits of journaling, such as enhancing self-awareness and identifying harmful or ineffective habits and behavior patterns.

You can use lists for many purposes: generating ideas, tracking tasks, identifying traits or attributes of people and objects, word associations, and so on.

Other structured journaling forms may include tables for habit tracking and graphs to track progress toward goals.

Drawing on your creative side

It's important to remember that journaling isn't limited to writing. In fact, some of the most famous journal keepers (think Leonardo Da Vinci or Frida Kahlo) used their journals to sketch out ideas for inventions, sculpture, paintings, or scientific concepts.

While you begin or expand your journaling practice, try adding different forms of expression to your pages. You might be surprised by the richness and depth of your multimedia journal entries.

REMEMBER

Visual poems, paintings, collages, and ink drawings — with or without writing accompanying them — are all perfectly at home in a journal.

Journaling for specific purposes

Journals are often kept for dedicated purposes. For example, you can have a journal for cooking and recipes, another for inspirational ideas, and another for work projects. Whether you choose to keep one journal that contains all topics or keep a separate journal for each topic is completely up to you. Over time, depending on your lifestyle and needs, you can develop a journal-keeping system that works for you.

One common dedicated type of journal is a gratitude journal. This type of journal is used solely as a place to record things that you're grateful for. You can find out more about gratitude journaling in Chapter 9.

Trying Your Hand at Journaling

If you're new to journaling or just coming back to the practice after a hiatus, you might be wondering which journaling methods can work for you. Before jumping into any of the more detailed chapters on these approaches to journaling, why not give one a try?

Do This

Select one of the following prompts that most appeals to you and respond to it in the space provided. I've included prompts for structured and unstructured free-writing, list making, drawing, and gratitude.

>> Write the first thought that comes to your mind. Keep writing whatever occurs to you.

This prompt encourages unstructured, associative free-writing. If you enjoy writing to this type of prompt, you might want to check out Mindfulness Journaling, covered in Chapter 6.

>> Make a list of the things you want to remember about today. You can make this a simple list, or you can add additional details or notes for each item, such as why it's important or what you want to remember about it.

This way of journaling is similar to what you might write in your daily log in a Bullet Journal. To find out more about this method, turn to Chapter 7.

>> Write about an event (large or small) that occurred recently. Describe what happened, who else was involved, and what your emotional response to it was. What about this event sticks with you the most?

This Reflective Journaling prompt helps you begin to think about a life experience and consider its implications or meaning for you. You can take a deep dive into Reflective Journaling in Chapter 2.

>> Select an object in your home or office that's meaningful to you. Write about the object and why it's important. Include a sketch of the object.

Including drawing and other visual art is an example of Creative Journaling. If this prompt speaks to you, check out Chapter 8.

>> Write down ten things and/or people you're grateful to have in your life today.

This prompt is an example of a simple Gratitude Journaling technique. If this kind of journaling appeals to you, flip to Chapter 9 for more information about keeping a gratitude journal.

_____

_____

_____

_____

Chapter **2**

Discovering the Many Benefits of Journaling

The reason that so many people are drawn to journaling — and likely one of the reasons you're reading this book — is because journaling is so very beneficial and in so many ways. These benefits have been proven and documented many times, through decades of research.

From school children just learning to write to elderly adults, journaling has been shown to improve emotional, mental, and physical health. It can unleash creativity and enhance productivity. It's all in the How and the Why you use it.

In this chapter, I examine those benefits and provide an overview of the many reasons and ways to use journaling to gain the most from it. I also talk about some of the studies that have been conducted, but don't worry, I'm not going to bore you with a bunch of statistics. I just want you to know that the benefits outlined in this chapter aren't the stuff of folklore — they're real and backed by research.

Enhancing Your Well-Being

People who journal regularly report experiencing an enhanced sense of overall well-being. Moreover, many have gained tangible improvements to their emotional, mental, and physical health. In this section, I give an overview of how journaling can improve your health in each of these areas.

Emotional and mental health

The area that has been studied the most when it comes to journaling is emotional and mental health. You've probably heard that journaling is an inexpensive form of psychotherapy. Most sayings contain a seed of truth; in this case, the seed has grown into a tree.

Studies conducted in clinical and educational settings since the 1960s have shown the following mental and emotional effects of journaling:

>> Reduces stress and anxiety

>> Boosts feelings of well-being

>> Supports self-love and acceptance

>> Improves the ability to cope with grief, loss, and illness

>> Increases mental clarity

WARNING

I'm not saying that journaling should replace counseling or psychotherapy. Professional therapeutic services have benefits that journaling can't provide. And it would be irresponsible of me to suggest otherwise. In fact, when combined with conventional therapy, journaling has been shown to increase the effectiveness of the therapy.

Counseling and psychotherapy both focus on communicating thoughts and feelings in a safe environment. The counselor or therapist acts as a mirror and resource for the person being counseled. Like a mirror, they reflect your own words and emotions back to you so that you can see them more objectively. As a resource, they can provide guidance, wisdom, and access to additional resources.

REMEMBER

Journaling works in the same way that counseling does. It gives you a safe space to communicate your deepest thoughts and emotions. It acts like a mirror, reflecting back to you, in your own words, your feelings, thoughts, attitudes, beliefs, and behavioral patterns. When approached with curiosity and an open mind, journaling can help you become more self-aware and increase your ability to process and make meaning of life.

Journaling also helps you tap into your inner wisdom, your innate guidance — that inner-self who knows what you really need and want and, when listened to, can help you shift your well-being in a positive direction.

Physical health

Improved mental health may be reason enough to journal, but did you know that journaling has also been shown to benefit physical health?

Dr. Ira Progoff, one of the first psychologists to study and document the effects of journaling, found that in addition to decreasing stress, anxiety, and fear, journal writing for just 15 to 20 minutes, three to five times a week, was correlated with increasing immune system function and decreasing blood pressure. The journal writers in the study went to the doctor less often and just felt better overall.

A 2017 study published in *Psychosomatic Medicine: Journal of Biobehavioral Medicine* (Elsevier) found that those who kept journals during divorce had lower heart rates and higher heart rate variability — both indicators of good health. We can extrapolate from this that journaling could have the same benefits during any stressful loss or life transition.

Other studies have shown that journaling improves overall memory function by enhancing the brain's ability to intake, process, and retrieve information. And because of its positive effects on thinking, journaling has been used in educational settings to help students understand how to think more logically and analytically.

Supercharging Inspiration and Achievement

Because journaling is a safe and private activity, and lends itself well to delving into literally any topic or personal characteristic, it's an excellent tool for exploring creative inspiration, practicing creative skills, and finding creative solutions to any kind of problem.

Inspirational ideas have a tendency to blossom into projects. It follows that journaling is a natural (and effective) way to develop and manage your project-related goals and tasks.

In this section, I discuss some of the ways your journal can help you power up your creative inspiration and achieve more in your life.

Creativity

Have you ever awakened from a dream inspired by a ground-breaking idea? Or had a brilliant solution to a problem while performing a routine task such as doing the dishes or taking a shower? Creative ideas come to us at all times of the day and night — often when we're thinking about something else entirely.

In addition to using words to capture feelings and ideas, you can use your journal as a sketchbook to create mind maps, detail visual ideas, and express emotions through forms and colors. You can also use it to record those inspired dreams.

TIP

Your journal is a place to capture ideas when they happen and then explore them in more depth later, when you have time. Because it encourages capturing ideas and self-reflection, journaling can help you with your creative process, whether your art is painting, music, or writing itself.

One of your journal's greatest gifts is that it can be messy and unformed, and that's okay. In your journal, you can develop ideas privately, without the burden of having to "make something good." Your journal gives you a place to practice without pressure. Because of its judgement-free nature, your journal can help you build confidence in your craft, as well as create a rich resource of ideas that you can come back to over and over again.

If you're interested in journaling to enhance your creativity, Chapter 8 and Chapter 11 each take a deeper dive into the creative side of journaling.

ARTISTS WHO JOURNALED THEIR CREATIVE INSPIRATION

Artists have long used journals as a place to try out and develop their ideas. Along with writing about their intimate daily lives and artistic processes, they sketched and diagrammed in their journal pages to try out new concepts. Here are four artists whose journals were used to develop their inspiration and artistic vision:

- Leonardo da Vinci, Renaissance artist, used his journals to sketch extensive diagrams, drawings, and notes related to his inventions and works of art, as well as entries on topics ranging from astronomy to everyday tasks.

- Frida Kahlo, Mexican painter, explored her life and art, including her fears and dreams, in her journals, employing a unique blend of colorful images and writing.

- Janice Lowry, American visual artist, filled her journals with small drawings, collages, and writing about her art, her daily life, and current events.

- Jack Whitten, American abstract expressionist, documented the progress of his artistic style along with his creative struggles in his journals, which he called his "studio notes."

Productivity

Journaling can be an amazing tool for enhancing your efficiency and productivity. Your journal is a place to manage your projects, create goals, establish doable tasks and timelines, and track your progress. It works equally well for major or minor projects and for establishing new habits.

In Chapter 12 I talk about a variety of journaling techniques that can help you create, organize, and successfully achieve your goals.

Writing craft

If you like to write, and you dream of becoming a better writer, your journal is a wonderful playground in which to practice.

I think the biggest breakthrough for me as a writer — that moment I went from writer-wannabe to knowing I was a writer — came when I recognized that journaling was writing practice. And it was in my journal that I found my authentic writing voice.

Consider the following truths about your journal. It's safe and private, and nothing you write is open to criticism. You can write from your heart, and your inner critic and editor — that voice in your head that's constantly belittling your writing and telling you that you're not a real writer — isn't welcome. Your journal is a playground, and you can put together words however you want in this playground.

You don't have to worry about spelling or punctuation, or whether your sentences flow coherently from one to the next. You can be as messy or neat as you want, and there's no one to say otherwise.

For example, you can use your journal to

>> Brainstorm plots

>> Develop characters

>> Sketch a scene

>> Practice dialogue

>> Create poetry

>> Explore points of view

>> Piece together story ideas

REMEMBER

Writing is writing, whether it's in your journal or in text or e-mail. The more you write from your heart — which journaling encourages and helps you practice — the more authentic all your writing becomes.

Improving Your Life

While you begin your exploration and practice of journaling, keep in mind the many ways you can use it to improve your life. More than a simple repository of feelings, or a mind dump, journaling with purpose and intention can help you make important personal gains.

When you treat it like a diary, you can use your journal to document small and large events in your life. You can explore your reactions and thoughts about those events — or just life, in general — which can help you increase self-awareness.

Or you can use your journal as a place to write down all your confusing thoughts and emotions in order to gain perspective, better understand your triggers, and decide what's truly important to you.

These are just two of the virtually unlimited ways that you can employ your journal, many of which you can read about in the following sections.

Recording events

An *event* is something that happens in a specific moment in time that creates an experience. An event can be planned or unplanned. It can involve interactions with other people, animals, or even objects.

Events can range from the mundane, such as receiving e-mails or making hair appointments, to the significant, such as weddings, accidents, or winning the lottery.

How many and what types of events you choose to write about in your journal is entirely up to you. Here are some things to consider when deciding which events to write about:

>> **Day-to-day life:** Do you want to be able to review past months and years in order to gain perspective on the general flow of your life? If so, then keeping track of regular appointments, such as haircuts and when you got your car serviced, can be enlightening when you want to evaluate the time you've spent on these types of activities. And it can be useful to know how many times you visited doctors and other healthcare providers and for what reasons.

>> **Emotional impact:** Do you intend to use your journal primarily to explore emotions and to make meaning of important events and relationships in your life? In this case, limiting your events to those that impact you emotionally makes the most sense.

Do you want to both keep track of everyday happenings and the bigger, life-impacting ones? There's no reason you can't do both.

Clarifying thoughts and feelings

You might want to start journaling in order to clarify the confusing thoughts and feelings that you have swirling around in you. Journaling is an amazing tool for making your thoughts and feelings more visible to you. The self-awareness and understanding you gain can give you the foundation needed to make significant and positive changes in your life.

Here are a few ways that journaling accomplishes this magic:

>> **Slowing down:** Writing down your feelings forces you to slow down in order to articulate and describe them. This slower pace helps you better understand your emotions and the thoughts and belief systems behind them.

>> **Changing your perspective:** Writing down conflicting thoughts helps you see things from different perspectives, which can inspire new insights and even help to resolve those conflicts.

>> **Organizing:** Journaling aids in organizing your thinking. It supports you while you explore confusing situations to find clarity and purpose.

>> **Living with purpose.** Writing about your strengths and passions helps you become more clear about your purpose. And a life lived with purpose is stronger and more satisfying.

Making decisions

Making sound decisions can be difficult, especially when you're not clear on what you want or know the potential outcome of each direction you could take.

Journaling gives you a forum in which to explore needs, wants, priorities, and potential results of any decision you make.

Here are some of the reasons journaling can help you make better decisions:

>> **Clarity:** Journaling is one of the best ways to gain clarity about your true, inner feelings about life choices. When you gain clarity about your feelings and thoughts, you make better decisions because you understand what's truly important to you — and why it's important.

>> **Patterns:** When you write about decisions that you've made in the past and that you're currently making in your life, you shed light on your decision-making patterns and results. This insight allows you to understand whether these patterns are serving you and consider trying different methods for making decisions.

>> **Analysis:** You can include the research that you've done on the pros and cons of different options in your journal, along with your thoughts and reactions to what you've found.

>> **Reflection:** Your journal provides a record of the thought process and reasons for decisions you make along the way — an incredibly useful tool for review and reflection about your decisions over time.

Tapping into your inner wisdom

You might call it intuition, insight, guidance, or inner wisdom. What you call it doesn't matter, but being able to tap into the deep part of you that knows what's truly right for you in any moment in time is one of the ways journaling can provide a stronger sense of purpose and help you be more confident in your decision making.

In order to tap into that inner wisdom or guidance, you need to be able to quiet yourself, let go of your fears and anxieties, let go of attachment to outcomes, and really listen to that inner voice.

That's not an easy task. Your inner critic may be shouting too loudly about how and why you don't deserve to receive anything nice or how you're not good enough to achieve something you want. Or maybe fear and anxiety have you paralyzed, unable to think, let alone listen.

REMEMBER

Journaling cuts through barriers to listening to your inner wisdom because the very act of writing can calm you, declutter your whirling thoughts, and help you confront the negative voices in your head. Writing your thoughts and feelings gives you the ability to quiet your mind and bring you into the present moment — where you're able to listen.

When you pour your dreams, visions, doubts, and fears onto the pages of your journal, along with all the negative self-talk, journaling begins to peel away any layers of resistance you have. Eventually, while you keep writing, your inner wisdom surfaces.

If you're interested in understanding more about how to access your inner wisdom, check out Chapter 6, as well as Chapter 13.

Discovering your Self

Every person has both an outer- and inner-self. The outer self is who you present to the world — you, on your best behavior. This is the self who holds back expressing thoughts, feelings, and behaviors that others might judge negatively. The outer-self is mostly concerned with how you're viewed by others, dressing and communicating appropriately so that you have a better chance of fitting in with your social and work groups.

When I talk about *Self* with a capital S, I'm referring to your inner-self, that deep inner emotional/spiritual part of you — the person you really are on the inside. The part of you that contains inner wisdom. The you who's creative and uninhibited, honest and vulnerable. The you who also has a dark side — who can be angry, depressed, or in pain — that you don't always want to see.

There's nothing wrong with having these outer and inner expressions of who you are. It's part of being human. But if your outer- and inner-selves aren't both aligned with your core values, you can feel conflicted and stressed.

For example, have you ever acted in a way or done something because of social (peer) pressure that you felt uncomfortable with or felt guilty about later? That discomfort is the tension between your outer- and inner-selves — between your words or actions, and what you truly value.

Here are some ways that journaling can help you discover your Self and then assist you with aligning your inner and outer ways of being:

>> **Identifying inner conflicts and influences:** Using writing to explore the tension and discomfort you feel in those conflicted situations can help you identify the influences in your life that don't support your values.

>> **Increasing confidence:** Putting your values and dreams in writing increases your confidence to live the life you want.

>> **Acknowledging your darkness:** Expressing your darker emotions and thoughts on the page allows you to bring light, compassion, and healing to the part of you that you hide from the world (and sometimes yourself).

>> **Being your Self:** The self-awareness you gain from journaling can help you align and integrate your inner and outer personas so that you can be your authentic Self in the world.

REMEMBER

When you have a strong sense of Self, you're not easily swayed by others' opinions or by *groupthink* — a forced or manipulated conformity to group ethics, values, and viewpoints. You're self-aware; you have a sense of purpose and know what's important to you. And you behave in ways that are consistent with your core values.

For methods and ideas related to journaling for self-development and discovery, turn to Chapters 6 and 13.

IN THIS CHAPTER

» **Understanding your reasons for journaling**

» **Creating realistic expectations for your journaling practice**

» **Deciding between journaling by hand or computer**

» **Collecting your journaling tools**

» **Setting up your journaling space**

Chapter **3**

Preparing for Your Journaling Practice

I f you're new to journaling or coming back to it after a long time, having a firm understanding of your motivations for journaling can help you set realistic goals and timeframes for getting started.

Can you journal without goals? Absolutely. However, I've found that knowing what you want to gain from journaling contributes to a more intentional approach to it. And the more intentional you are, the greater the benefits.

To help you identify your underlying motivations, the first part of this chapter can help you articulate and explore your reasons for journaling, as well as what's most important to you. You then have the foundation from which to approach your goals and make choices about when and how much you want to journal.

After you understand your reasons for journaling, it becomes easier to select the right tools and set up a space that best supports you when you begin.

Exploring Your Reasons for Journaling

Do you have a clear idea of what attracted you to this book?

Perhaps you've been hearing about journaling for a while and wonder how it might benefit you. Maybe you used to journal and want to get back into it. Or you've been journaling for a long time and hope to find ways to renew or deepen your practice.

Whatever the urge that prompted you to open these pages, having a solid grasp of your underlying motivations and the ability to articulate your reasons for journaling can strengthen your confidence and help your journaling practice get off to a good start.

Listing your reasons

You might not really know why you're interested in journaling, or, conversely, you might have a whole jumble of ideas about why you want to start or resume a journaling practice. To gain clarity for yourself on what's motivating you, I recommend brainstorming a list of all the reasons that you want to journal. For example, a list might include

>> Record my daily events.

>> Write about my important childhood memories.

>> Understand myself better.

>> Have a private place to express my deepest emotions.

>> Play with poetry.

>> Create and track my life goals.

» Think "out loud" on the page to improve how I make decisions.

Do This

Write your list in the space provided. Feel free to borrow some of the reasons from the preceding example list, or refer back to the benefits and uses described in Chapter 2 that resonate with you. Keep listing until you run out of ideas.

Keep this list handy. The following section helps you narrow down your reasons to your top three priorities.

Identifying your top priorities

If you're like most people, you can think of many reasons for wanting to journal. When starting a journaling practice with intentionality, narrow down those reasons to your top three to help you focus on what's most important to you.

Do This

To identify your top three reasons for journaling, review the list you wrote in the preceding section. Out of all the reasons you listed, which ones would you be absolutely *thrilled* about achieving as a result of your journaling practice?

For example, although I might want to play with poetry in my journal, I'd be *really* happy if I succeeded in writing out my most important childhood memories and how they influenced who I am today.

Circle your top three, most exciting reasons and write them out again here:

_____

_____

_____

Keep these reasons — your journaling goals — while you establish your journaling practice. They will help you choose the journaling method(s) that are most likely to provide the benefits you're looking for. And, for additional guidance, you can read about and get some practice with five different types of journaling in Part 2 of this book.

Setting Realistic Expectations for Your Journaling Practice

Setting realistic expectations helps ensure that you'll be more satisfied with your journaling practice. It's easy in the beginning to be overly enthusiastic and expect more from yourself than your life can accommodate. If you expect to journal an hour every day, and then your job and other responsibilities get in the way so that you don't manage to journal as planned, you might feel like you're failing and give up on the idea of maintaining a journaling practice. Or you might avoid journaling altogether when you know you won't have a full hour, essentially setting yourself up to fail.

It's natural to feel disappointed when you don't meet your lofty expectations. Being real about what you can do is the key to getting it done.

REMEMBER

Being realistic doesn't mean being pessimistic. Pessimism would say, "Have you seen my life? There's no way I can maintain a regular journaling practice. I might as well give up before I get started." Realism responds to Pessimism with, "I know what is and isn't possible, and I'm sure I can set a reasonable expectation that I'll be able to handle. I just need to think through the logistics."

Figuring out your ideal journaling schedule

Deciding how often and how much time you want to journal is a choice that is unique to each person, depending on many life variables. Consider the following questions when determining the best journaling schedule for your lifestyle:

» Is it easy for you to focus quickly on a task, or does it take a while for you to settle into it?

» Do you like spending time alone?

» Do you enjoy extended periods of introspection, or do you get restless after a few minutes?

» Is your daily schedule already full, and is it difficult for you to find time for new pursuits?

» Is it easy or difficult for you to find uninterrupted time during a normal day?

» Do you have more time on some days than others? If so, which days would be best for taking time to journal?

» Do you prefer a regular routine, or are you comfortable with a varied routine?

» How much time do you *want* to journal, compared with how much time you think you'll be *able* to journal?

>> If you had no time constraints, which of the following time-periods would you prefer to journal: 10 minutes, 20 minutes, 30 minutes, or 1 hour?

After thinking through the answers to those questions, you probably have a pretty good, realistic idea of how often and for how long you want to journal. If so, congratulations! Proceed to the following Do This prompt. Not sure? Have no fear. The following section, "Building incrementally for achievable results," discusses how to divide your time to make it easier to start a sustainable journaling practice.

ESTABLISHING A NEW DAILY HABIT

Starting new habits is easiest when done incrementally, in small chunks. Consider this little example from my own life.

Although floss has been around since the 1800s, flossing teeth wasn't a widespread, daily part of Americans' self-care routine until the 1970s. Those of us who were raised prior to that time had to incorporate it into our lives as a new habit — something I struggled with for years.

No matter how often my dentist exhorted me or how much I wanted to, I couldn't seem to remember to floss my teeth! After each visit to the dentist, I would floss for a few days and then soon forget again.

My turning point occurred when I lowered my expectations by breaking down my goal behavior into smaller, easily achievable behaviors. My ideal was to floss every day. I decided that one day a week was better than none and that I would floss every Monday evening before bed. I put a reminder on my calendar and — what do you know? — it worked. After I had successfully flossed every Monday for six weeks, I added Wednesday. Then Friday. And soon thereafter, I was flossing every day.

The moral of this story is that when a new habit or goal feels too hard or overwhelming, break it down into easily achievable actions and work your way up, action by action, toward your goal.

Do This

Use the following entries to record your preferred journaling schedule.

How often I want to journal:

_____

How much time I want to spend in each journaling session:

_____

_____

REMEMBER

What you write in the preceding activity is a starting point and not set in stone. You may want to adjust your timeframes for the different types of journaling you do or your different reasons for journaling.

Building incrementally for achievable results

TIP

No matter what expectations you've set for yourself and your journaling practice, you can be more successful when you start small and work your way toward your ideal goal.

Firming up frequency

Think about how often you want to journal. (Not sure? Refer to the section "Figuring out your ideal journaling schedule," earlier in this chapter, for assistance.) I list several frequency options in Table 3-1 and, for each option, a commitment plan to get started.

After you achieve your commitment for at least a month, then gradually increase your number of days until you reach your goal.

Honing in on how much time to journal

Consider how many minutes you want to journal during each session. (The section "Figuring out your ideal journaling schedule," earlier in this chapter, helps you decide.)

TABLE 3-1

How Often You Want to Journal

How Often	How to Get Started
Daily	Commit to 3 days per week, evenly spaced, according to what will work best with your schedule; for example, Monday, Wednesday, Friday; or Tuesday, Thursday, Sunday.
Weekdays	Commit to 2 to 3 days per week, evenly spaced.
3 times per week	Select which 3 days you want to journal, but start by committing to just 2 days per week. Use your 3rd day as a backup day, in case you miss one of the other days.
Weekly	I don't recommend committing to less than one day per week. Select the day of the week you want to journal and one alternate day, in case you miss the selected day.
Randomly, when you feel like it and have time	Because you want to build a practice, it should be more intentional. Select one of the other plans above and make a commitment to yourself.
Other: In the section "Figuring out your ideal journaling schedule," earlier in this chapter, did you write down something other than the frequencies listed above?	Commit to journaling on half to two-thirds of the number of days you decided on. Then, select alternate, backup days, in case you miss a planned day.

TIP

To get started, I recommend cutting your desired time in half. So, if you wrote down 30 minutes, commit to 15; 20 minutes, commit to 10; and so on, with a minimum of 5 minutes to start. Breaking down your journaling goals into smaller, easily achievable actions makes them feel easier to accomplish. As you grow in confidence, and journaling becomes a regular part of your life, you can increase the length of time and/or frequency of your sessions.

Choosing Your Main Medium

There are two primary ways to journal:

>> By hand (analog)

>> Using a computer or app (digital)

Many people come to journaling with a clear preference for one of these. If you're new to journaling, you might be curious about which mode can work best for you.

There are pros and cons to both methods, which I discuss in the following sections. Consider these factors when deciding which type of media you want to start with.

Journaling by hand: Arguments for and against

Many people assume that journaling is always done by hand. For me, the primary advantage of journaling by hand is that your journal and writing instruments are inexpensive and portable. However, there are disadvantages, including that your journal might not be safe from prying eyes, loss, or natural disasters.

Consider the following advantages and disadvantages before you decide for yourself.

The pros of analog journaling

There are many reasons that journaling by hand is preferred by the majority of journal keepers. Some of the most compelling reasons include

>> **Memory and comprehension:** The sensory-motor coordination involved in handwriting activates more parts of the brain than typing does, while also slowing cognitive processing. The benefits of this increased brain activity include improved memory and deeper comprehension of concepts.

When journaling by hand, these benefits may enhance your ability to gain insights while journaling reflectively. (Turn to Chapter 5 for an overview of the reflective journaling method.)

- » **Stress reduction:** The very act of writing by hand can reduce stress. This stress reduction occurs, in part, because you have to slow down your thought processes while you write, giving it a meditative quality.

- » **Simplicity:** A paper journal is simple. It's cheap, portable, and doesn't depend on batteries.

- » **Enjoyment:** For those who prefer the tactile feeling, writing on paper can be a more enjoyable experience than journaling on an electronic device.

The cons of analog journaling

In spite of its popularity and benefits, there are also reasons that journaling by hand might not be your ultimate choice. Analog journaling is

- » **Messy:** For those who write slowly or whose hands tend to cramp or smear ink (I'm thinking of us lefties), writing by hand can be messy and sometimes painful.

- » **Not versatile:** You can't include multimedia, such as audio or video recordings, and attaching pictures is complicated. Also, it's time-consuming and challenging to search for specific content, create a backup, or convert the contents to another format.

- » **Hard to edit:** It's difficult to make clean corrections, and copying and pasting requires additional tools.

- » **Less private:** From a privacy perspective, analog is less safe than digital. Even if you lock your notebook in a safe, your journal is subject to being found and read by someone else. So you need to rely on the integrity of those around you.

- » **Not physically safe:** An analog journal is also less safe from loss or disaster, such as fires and floods, while a digital journal can be easily backed up to the cloud or another device.

MY LITTLE STUDY OF JOURNALING BY HAND VERSUS COMPUTER

I once ran a small experiment to find out which method — digital or analog — was more effective. I asked a group of participants to journal exclusively using a computer for one week and then by hand the following week. During the third week, they blended both methods.

At the start, about a third of the participants said that they preferred handwriting, a quarter preferred journaling digitally, and the remaining participants had no preference.

At the end of the three-weeks, I gave everyone a survey about the quality of their entrie. Overall, handwriting scored slightly higher on description, exploring thoughts and attitudes, insights, and expressing profound truths, while digital journaling scored higher on tracking daily activities and goals, and linear thinking.

Everyone expressed surprise at discovering benefits to whichever mode they didn't usually use. For example, those who preferred handwriting at the start ended up liking journaling digitally more than they thought they would, and those who originally preferred digital journaling found writing by hand more satisfying than they expected.

The conclusion? Whether you journal by hand or computer is mostly up to personal preference, but there are benefits to trying both.

Going digital: Comparing advantages and disadvantages

Over time, with improvements in electronic platforms and applications, and new generations of adults raised with digital smartphones and other devices, digital journaling has become more widely accepted and popular.

Like analog journaling, there are both pros and cons to digital journaling. I provide the following lists for both sides of the argument to help you determine what may work best for you.

The advantages of digital journaling

Check out the following list of advantages to digital journaling:

>> **Ease of use:** A digital journal can be easier to organize and manage than a paper one.

>> **Physical safety:** Because it can be stored in multiple places (in the cloud, as well as on a hard drive), your digital journal can be safe from loss and natural disasters.

>> **Privacy:** Definitely a pro of the digital journal. You can password protect and double authenticate access to it.

>> **Access:** If you carry a smartphone, your digital journal is available to you everywhere you go, making it easy to add notes throughout the day, whereas, you might not always want to tote your paper journal around.

>> **Versatility:** You can include digital multimedia in your journal entries: audio, video, images, and so on.

>> **Speed:** If you type quickly, or use speech to text technology, it can be easier to pour out your thoughts and emotions onto the page because you don't have to slow down as much.

>> **Editing capabilities:** You can freely correct errors, copy, paste, and rearrange your writing.

>> **Therapeutic value:** Exploring your thoughts and emotions through digital entry — including typing, speech to text, and using a digital pen — can provide the same therapeutic value as handwriting.

The disadvantages of digital journaling

The following list outlines reasons you might not prefer digital journaling:

>> The primary disadvantage to digital journaling is that keyboarding tends to encourage linear, rather than associative/creative thinking. However, that disadvantage may be overcome by using a digital pen, combined with a handwriting or drawing application.

- **Expense:** Digital journals require a device, such as computer, smartphone, or tablet, all of which cost more than a paper notebook.

- **Energy:** A digital journal requires power from some source, such as batteries (and you need the ability to recharge those batteries).

- **Emotional distance:** Because of the technical nature of typing and working within software limitations, digital journaling can distance you from your emotions when compared with writing by hand.

- **Risk of loss:** If you don't back up your journal to the cloud or a hard drive, you run the risk of losing all of your journal entries forever if something should happen to the device on which it's stored.

- **Not tactile:** Journaling on a computer or other digital device might not feel as pleasurable, from a tactile perspective.

Figuring out what works best for you

Read through the lists in the preceding sections. Do any pros or cons stand out for you?

Maybe there's just one item that's a deal clincher — the enhanced privacy of digital journaling, for example. Or the ability to copy and paste. Or perhaps you don't like computers and love the tactile feeling of pen on paper. Whichever method you use, the choice is deeply personal.

TIP

If you're still not sure which mode to use, I recommend starting out with the one that seems easiest. You can always switch — or even blend modes — later on.

Gathering Your Tools

One of the attractive aspects of journaling is that it doesn't require a lot of equipment or tools for you to get started. In the following sections, I describe the minimum supplies you want to have on hand.

While you expand the ways in which you journal, you may want to add to your journaling toolbox. But, for now, keep things simple so that you can focus on your journaling practice, instead of the technology or tools.

Choosing a nifty notebook

Planning to journal by hand? Get a notebook dedicated for that purpose.

TIP

If you're just starting out or feel at all nervous about the idea of writing out your thoughts and feelings, I strongly suggest keeping it simple: Buy an inexpensive spiral bound, college-ruled notebook. An 8.5-x-11-inch notebook is fine. If you want to be able to carry your journal in a purse or briefcase, then pick up an A5 (5.5-x-8.25-inch) notebook.

If you prefer that your notebooks feel special, you can choose one that has a decorative or hard cover.

WARNING

I typically discourage spending money on journals that have expensive bindings and paper because it can feel intimidating to "spoil" the beautiful paper with messy handwriting — or fill that gorgeous leather journal with equally messy feelings.

Picking a comfortable writing instrument

After your journal notebook (see the preceding section), your writing instrument is the next big choice. The best pen or pencil to use is different for each person.

If you already have a favorite writing instrument, skip to the section "Optional writing tools," later in this chapter.

Pens

I recommend using an inexpensive ballpoint pen to start — preferably fine or medium point, in blue or black ink. There are many brands to choose from in this category.

The pen needs to fit comfortably in your hand and be easy to hold and write with for long periods of time without your fingers cramping. (If you haven't done a lot of handwriting lately, you may need to experiment with several pens before you find the right one for you.)

TIP

If you have trouble with ink smearing on the page, as I do because of the way I write with my left hand, look for pens labeled "smudge-proof," "no smear," or "non-smudge."

Pencils

The advantage of writing with a pencil is that you can make corrections — something that's rather difficult to do with a pen.

You can use any lead pencil. But, to avoid the irritation of constantly having to sharpen it, I suggest using a mechanical pencil — as long as you don't have a tendency to press down hard while writing, in which case, the lead will break often.

Like a pen (discussed in the preceding section), the main criteria for your mechanical pencil is that it feels comfortable to write with for long periods of time.

Optional writing tools

You may want to have on hand a few of the following writing tools. These are optional, but they can add some spice and playfulness to your journal writing:

>> Crayons

>> Colored markers or pencils

>> Gel pens in a variety of colors

>> Colored highlighters

I discuss additional art-oriented journaling tools in detail in Chapter 8.

Selecting a digital journaling application

Planning to journal digitally? The sheer number of applications to choose from can seem overwhelming. However, to make it easier, you can think about the apps as falling into three main categories: word processing, note-taking, and journaling-dedicated.

In the following sections, I list some of the most commonly used and highest rated digital journaling apps. Which you choose to use depends on availability, price, and personal preferences. I encourage you to experiment until you find the app that works best for you.

Word processors

You most likely already have access to at least one of these applications. They're easy to use — just open a document, title with a date, and start typing. Formatting options are powerful, you can add images, and your journal documents can be safely stored with password protection applied on any online service such as Dropbox or OneDrive:

>> Microsoft Word

>> Apple Pages

>> Google Docs

Note-taking apps

Note-taking apps are great for journaling because you can enter a new note for each day, and the app automatically creates a table of contents for your entries.

Most note-taking apps also allow you to title your entries, apply tags, and include links to web pages, images, and sometimes other media such as video and audio. They're also automatically password protected — either by having to log into the app or to your device to access the app.

Here are a few that I've used or that come highly recommended by others:

- **>> Evernote:** Subscription-based app that has a free version capable of handling your journaling needs. It's cross platform and works on just about every device and also on the web, so you can work with it online or offline (connected or not connected) and your entries sync between devices.

- **>> Microsoft OneNote:** Comes with Microsoft's Office 365 subscription package, but you can also get it for free on almost any platform. OneNote has a binder-like interface, which you might find appealing.

- **>> Apple Notes:** Included free on all Mac devices, this app is simple to use. You can include images and password-protect individual entries.

- **>> Notion:** Powerful online-only note-taking app that also has database features.

Journaling-dedicated apps

Journaling-dedicated applications can encourage you to journal frequently. Some are online only, meaning you have to have the Internet to access them, while others are cross-platform and can be accessed both on- and offline, with automatic syncing between devices. Some journaling apps provide prompts and have other journaling-specific features. Most of these apps have free plans or trial subscriptions, making them easy to try out.

Here are some of the most popular apps:

- **>> Day One:** Subscription-based, cross-platform journaling app that allows for unstructured, free-form journaling. Features include tagging, advanced security, export, and backup options.

- **>> Penzu:** Offers both free and paid plans. Options include different background colors, journal covers, security, and custom reminders.

- **>> Daybook:** Free cloud-based app that has a minimalist interface.

- **>> Journey.cloud:** Popular app that has both free and paid subscription plans, but you need to pay for advanced formatting and other functions.

» **Momento:** Designed to capture moments in your life, you can use this app for journaling, add images and video content, pull in content from your social media, and search entries. Offers both free and paid monthly subscription plans.

» **WriteMore.io:** Online-only journaling and writing app designed to encourage daily journaling. This application is free for all new users at the time this book went to press. Provides journaling and creative-writing prompts on demand.

Preparing Your Journaling Space

You have all your tools (discussed in the section "Gathering Your Tools," earlier in this chapter), you're clear on why you want to journal (flip back to the section "Exploring Your Reasons for Journaling," earlier in this chapter, if you need some help with your motivations), and have established reasonable expectations for yourself (see the section "Setting Realistic Expectations for Your Journaling Practice," earlier in this chapter). You're ready to start journaling, right?

Not quite.

Where you choose to set up your journaling space will affect how you journal.

Carving out your niche

You need a private, dedicated space in which to journal in order to be able to think and reflect without interruption. Ideally, your space should promote a sense of calm. It should be quiet, away from the beaten path, and private. After all, the last thing you want is someone looking over your shoulder while you're pouring your heart onto the page, or to be constantly interrupted while attempting to focus.

If you already have an at-home office or a separate room that you can retreat to for journaling, skip to the following section.

If you don't have access to a separate space, consider turning a closet into a mini-office. Or you can create a dedicated space by setting off a corner of a living room or bedroom by using a divider.

The point of having a dedicated journaling space is to protect your privacy and help you feel safe and able to focus and express yourself meaningfully. Remember, this is *your* time. Give yourself the time and space you deserve.

Getting comfy with the right furnishings

Some people prefer a big, overstuffed chair or recliner to sit in while journaling. Others like to sit at a writing desk. I like to journal on a lap desk while sitting on a soft rocking chair I have in a corner of my office.

Decide what seating arrangement would be the most conducive to your journaling, and then furnish your space with a comfortable chair — don't skimp on the comfort! — and a flat surface on which to journal. If you're sitting at a desk, make sure your chair is set up ergonomically to reduce physical strain.

Seeing the light

I can't overemphasize the importance of good lighting. Whether you're journaling by hand or digitally, avoid dim or harsh overhead lighting. Either type of lighting can induce eye strain and fatigue.

Natural lighting is best, so if you plan to journal during the day, you might consider situating your journaling space near a window. You also want a good quality lamp that has a daylight-simulating lightbulb for journaling when the sun's not up.

Setting the stage with the right props

Think about other ways to make your journaling space feel extra comfy and special. Consider adding some of the following props to make your space feel attractive and to encourage introspection and reflection:

>> Candles

>> Pen/pencil holder

>> Side table and coaster for coffee or tea

>> Bluetooth speaker, if you like to set the mood with music

>> An indoor plant for soothing greenery (if you have the room)

Most importantly, do what feels good to you. If you prefer a minimalist environment, and this list seems like too much stuff, you can stick with the basic tools.

REMEMBER

When all is said and done, the best space is the one that makes you want to sit down and journal.

Chapter **4**

Establishing Your Practice

L ike all healthy habits, making journaling a regular practice takes structuring your life for success. It means making space for writing amidst all of your other daily (or near daily) responsibilities and routines. Because, even when you enjoy and *want* to journal, starting any new habit can prove difficult.

In this chapter, I provide guidance on how to best define your structure and create your individualized plan. There's even a special activity, "Writing Your Plan," at the end of this chapter to support your journaling practice. You may think this process makes a big to-do about something as simple as journaling, but trust me, when you structure your life to allow for and support your writing time, you can integrate journaling into your life more easily.

Making Time for Journaling

The first step to making journaling a regular part of your life is to examine your schedule in order to make time for journaling. And I mean *make* time, not *find* time — "finding" implies that you already have the time, a sliver of a gap between other activities, just waiting for you to fill it in.

In my experience, when you attempt to fit in a new activity without restructuring your existing routine, you're setting yourself up for failure. Or, at the very least, for struggle. Instead, you want to *make* time — carve out a space by either moving other activities around or giving up something else that you don't see as a priority or that you want to stop doing anyway.

TIP

Try pairing journaling with an activity that you love to do, which will provide a natural positive reinforcement for your new writing practice. Studies have shown that people form new habits more easily when the new behaviors are rewarded with other pleasurable activities.

For example, one student of mine (I'll call her Victoria) liked to read in bed for 30 minutes before turning out the light each night. She wanted to add journaling to her nighttime routine and realized that she needed to make some adjustments. So, she decided to start going to bed 15 minutes earlier. She journaled for 15 minutes and then rewarded herself with reading. That way, too, she could be flexible with her time. If she chose to write for 20 minutes rather than 15, she simply shortened her reading time by the same number of minutes. This arrangement worked quite well for Victoria, and it wasn't long before journaling and reading became a paired habit.

Deciding when to write

Journaling is flexible, so you can choose any time to write that works for you. In addition, you don't have to write every day, if you prefer a different schedule. Each person is unique, and you have to discover what best suits you. Be patient with yourself because it may take some trial and error before you find your ideal journaling routine.

THE BENEFITS OF MAKING A PLAN

Why go to all the trouble of creating a plan for establishing your journaling practice? Here are a few known benefits of having a plan:

- Enhances your peace of mind
- Makes you more likely to take action and achieve your goal
- Ultimately saves you time
- Helps you keep your priorities in order
- Improves self-awareness and self-confidence

Taking the time to make a plan may seem inconvenient, especially when you're in a hurry to get started. But any journey is easier when you have a map that shows you how to get where you're going — whether that journey is literal or metaphorical.

REMEMBER

You decide when you want to write. Arrange your schedule to give yourself quality time.

Start by considering a normal week in your life, and answer the following questions:

» What time do you usually get up, eat breakfast, and start your day? If you're wide awake in the mornings, could you get up 15 minutes earlier to write and still get enough sleep?

» If you have more energy in the evenings, could you adjust your bedtime by 15 minutes, in either direction, to make time to write?

» If you have a job, could you schedule a regular journaling time during the workday, such as at lunch or during a break?

» If your days aren't all the same, could you schedule journaling before or after a regular daily activity, such as waking, mealtime, or exercise?

>> How often do you want to write? Daily or several times a week?

>> What about your days off work? Do you want to journal on those days?

>> What activities do you find most pleasurable, or what do you do to wind down? Which of these activities could you turn into a self-reward for journaling?

>> What activities do you want to do less? Could you substitute journaling?

After you consider the questions in the preceding list, along with your preferences, write down the frequency and time you plan to write. The section "Writing Your Plan," later in this chapter, provides space for you to log this info.

REMEMBER

It may take a bit of trial and error before you discover what works best for you. You're not locked into this decision forever. If you find that "before breakfast" is just not happening, then reconsider your schedule and decide on another time that can support your success.

Putting it on the calendar

After you figure out when you want to journal (discussed in the preceding section), put it on your calendar.

WARNING

Don't skip this step! If you don't write journaling into your day, you can more easily procrastinate or skip your journaling time altogether.

So, right now, pull out your calendar — paper or digital, it doesn't matter — and set an appointment for each day in the coming week when you want to journal. If you didn't establish a specific time, set an approximate time based on the usual adjoining activity. For example, if you normally go to the gym after work, usually around 6:00 p.m., then set your journaling time for 6:00 and your gym start at 6:15 or 6:30.

Setting reminders

If you make your journaling appointments (see the preceding section) in a digital calendar, set an alert to pop up 15 minutes before your appointed time. With this reminder, you get enough time to finish up what you're doing, shift gears mentally, and gather your journaling supplies.

If you wrote your journaling appointments on a paper calendar, you need to get creative about how to set a reminder:

>> Use a reminder app on your smartphone or watch.

>> A strategically placed yellow sticky note (or notes) can work if you don't use apps or any smart devices.

>> If you have an accountability partner (see the following section), ask them to call you a few minutes before your journaling time.

Holding yourself accountable

After you go to all the work to make time in your routine for journaling (flip back to the section "Deciding when to write," earlier in this chapter), hold yourself accountable so that you stick to your schedule.

For some naturally structured people, accountability is easy. But most people don't fall into that category and need some coaxing to get and maintain motivation.

TIP

To coax yourself to adhere to your journaling schedule, include positive reinforcement in your plan. You can reserve a pleasurable activity as a reward for sticking with your writing time. Maybe you get to watch another episode of your favorite TV series or take a nice hot bath after you write.

Establishing an *accountability buddy* — another person whom you agree to report to regarding whether you journaled as intended — can help you force yourself to be accountable. If you have an accountability buddy, make it a two-way street. Buddy up with someone who's going to report (or who already is reporting) back to you regarding a habit that they're trying to establish.

Setting Boundaries

Do you live with children, other family members, or roommates who assume you're always available? Or maybe you have coworkers or a boss who expect you to always put work before your personal needs. If you find yourself in either (or both) of those situations, you need to set boundaries around your journaling time.

In this context, a *boundary* is a limit or space that you put between you and another person — where your needs end and theirs begin. Healthy boundaries for journaling include

>> Having time to yourself without being interrupted

>> Expecting your privacy to be respected — particularly when you're using a paper journal, which is usually more vulnerable to snooping than a digital one

>> Remaining free from others' controlling or manipulative behaviors

You may feel that others' needs should come before yours. However, just like when you're flying on an airplane and the attendant instructs the adults to secure their own oxygen masks before their children's, you can't take care of others unless you first take care of yourself.

REMEMBER

Give yourself permission to do what's best for you. Your journaling time is part of your self-care. If you value your time and yourself, others will, too.

Announcing your intentions

When you decide to set boundaries, let those close to you know your plans. Tell them that you need to take some time for yourself, when you plan to take it, and for how long. Be clear that you expect them to respect your time and that you don't want anything (short of an emergency) to interrupt you.

Making arrangements for childcare and other responsibilities

If you don't set boundaries related to your availability, family members or work responsibilities may attempt to interfere with your writing time. Make contingency plans and provide guidance. For example

>> If you have young children, ask another adult in your household to supervise them during your journaling time. Consider paying a teenager to watch them. Or choose a time to write when your children are sleeping or in daycare. If your children are older, think about what they might need during your time. Let them know what they should do if they want a snack, who to go to for permission, and so on so you have some uninterrupted writing time.

>> At home or work, hang up a Do Not Disturb sign and, if possible, lock the door while you're writing.

>> Silence your phone and let any calls go to voicemail. (See the "Turning off social media and other distractions" section later in this chapter for more ways to avoid interruptions.)

Holding the line

Inevitably, unless you live alone, *someone* will try to convince you to put their needs before yours. They may want you to do something that reduces your writing time, or they may try to interrupt you while you're journaling.

You can simply say no. Let them know that you value and respect their time and that you expect them to value and respect your time, as well. Unless it's a true emergency, whatever they want can wait.

Overcoming Fear and Other Obstacles to Journaling

It's time to talk about the metaphorical elephant in the room: fear. You may fear developing a journaling practice for reasons both internal and external. For example, here are some of the fears and barriers that clients have expressed to me over the years:

>> What if someone violates my privacy and reads my journal?

>> What if I start writing my negative thoughts and emotions, and I go down a dark rabbit hole?

>> I have small children who never sleep. I don't have any time to write!

>> I have too many responsibilities, and I have to put myself last.

>> I'm a procrastinator. I've tried journaling before, and I always end up putting it off.

>> I'm worried about becoming too self-involved if I spend time writing just for me.

>> I have a hard time finishing things, and I'm afraid I won't stay motivated.

>> I'm terrified of what I might see if I let my true self out onto the page.

Do you see yourself in any of these statements? If so, or if you have another barrier or fear not listed here, it's time to acknowledge it, face it, and make it your friend. (You can find a way to do just that in the section "Making your fear your friend," later in this chapter.) Because after you meet your fear face to face, you can move forward and make journal writing, and its many benefits, a rewarding part of your life.

Determining what's holding you back

If you are feeling fearful or doubtful about being able to start or maintain a journaling practice, it's useful to articulate the reasons for your fear or doubt. Once you've determined the things that are holding you back, you can find ways to address and overcome them.

Use the following prompt to help identify your fears about journaling and any other potential obstacles in your life.

Do This

Write a list of all the things that could go wrong or stand in the way of fulfilling your journaling and writing goals. Include any obstacles listed in the preceding section that apply to you.

Now, rate on a scale of 1 to 5 each item on the list based on whether you think it will actually happen, where 1 equals very unlikely and 5 equals very likely. Rating your list can help to calm some of your fears by understanding that those rated as 1s or 2s aren't likely to happen and are therefore irrational (see the discussion on rational versus irrational fear in the following section, "Facing your fear"). And you can address the more realistic, or rational, obstacles (those rated higher on the scale) first.

Facing your fear

A common barrier to journaling is fear. Whether the emotion is strong or mild, if you feel at all fearful about beginning a journaling practice, then the following sections may provide the help you need.

Categorizing fear: Rational or irrational

There are two types of fear: rational and irrational. Although both kinds of fear are natural and valid, and everyone experiences them, you need to understand the differences between the two. Once your fear is categorized and sorted out, you can journal without (or, at the very least, with less) anxiety.

The main difference between rational and irrational fear is the likelihood of whatever you fear coming true.

>> *Rational fear* occurs when your safety is being legitimately threatened. For example, if you're chased by a bear, you're afraid the bear might hurt you. And you have good reason to think so. Your likelihood of being hurt is high.

>> *Irrational fear* occurs even when there's no apparent link to a legitimate threat nor any immediate threat. For example, you're afraid of heights because you think you might fall, but if you're standing on a bridge or balcony that has a sturdy railing, the likelihood of you falling is low. You have very little chance of actually falling.

Both types of fear flood your body with adrenaline, engage the parts of your brain needed for survival, and activate a fight-or-flight response. Your heart rate increases to provide more oxygen to your muscles and brain. Your eyesight becomes sharper, and your digestive and reproductive systems slow down to provide more blood flow to the systems necessary for survival.

In the case of a rational fear, these physical responses make sense because you need to react to the threat. In the case of irrational fear, these responses create physical and emotional stress that has no outlet; there's no immediate threat and therefore nothing to respond to. The good news is that irrational fear can be addressed.

Uncovering the cause of your fear

The best way I know to overcome fear is to acknowledge and work with it. That means first discovering the core reason underlying the fear. The problem is that most of us hide the true cause of our fear under superficial reasons. It's a self-protection mechanism.

The following exercise can help you discover the underlying cause of your fear. Follow these steps yourself in the following Do This prompt:

1. **Begin by stating what it is about journaling that you're afraid of.**

   Example: *I'm afraid someone in my family will read my journal.*

2. **Complete this statement: If [my fear] happens, I'm afraid that [result] will happen.**

   Example: *If someone in my family reads my journal, I'm afraid that they'll be upset by what they read, especially if I write something negative about them.*

3. **Repeat Step 2, substituting whatever you wrote in the second blank in the position of the first blank.**

   Your new sentence reads, "If [result] happens, I'm afraid that [new result] will happen."

   Example: *If they're upset about what I've written, I'm afraid they'll judge me.*

4. **Repeat Step 3 until you uncover the core reason behind your fear.**

   Don't stop when you think you have the answer. Keep going, keep digging. What's the very worst thing that could happen if your fear came true? You know you've reached the core when you can't find any more reasons beneath the previously stated fear.

   Example: *If they judge me harshly, I'm afraid they won't want to talk to me again. And if they don't want to talk to me anymore, I'm afraid I'll lose them, lose their love. And if I lose their love, I'm afraid I'll be alone.*

You can only face your fear when you know what it is.

REMEMBER

TIP

If you find yourself reacting very strongly to this activity, you're not unusual. Take a moment to notice and acknowledge your reaction. ("My hands are shaking while I write this. I wonder why my hands are shaking?") Also express compassion to yourself. ("You're very brave for being willing to explore this fear.")

You don't ever have to continue if you feel uncomfortable. Simply acknowledge your choice to continue or not, without judgment, until you feel safe to try again.

Do This

Complete Steps 1 through 4 as described in the previous "Uncovering the cause of your fear" section; write your responses in the spaces provided.

I am afraid . . .

_____

_____

If _____ happens, I am afraid . . .

_____

_____

If _____ happens, I am afraid . . .

_____

_____

_____

_____

_____

_____

_____

_____

_____

_____

_____

_____

Keep writing until you reach your deepest underlying fear. Feel free to use a sheet of paper if you need more space to write.

When you've uncovered the core reason for your fear, the next step is not to fight it, but to make it your friend. I discuss how to do just that in the following section, "Making your fear your friend."

FINDING INSPIRATION FOR FACING FEAR

I find encouragement and motivation for overcoming fear in the words of great leaders, writers, and artists, past and present. Here are three quotes that I hope inspire you to gain courage.

"You gain strength, courage and confidence by every experience in which you really stop to look fear in the face. You are able to say to yourself, 'I have lived through this horror. I can take the next thing that comes along.' You must do the thing you think you cannot do."

— Eleanor Roosevelt, First Lady in the U.S from 1933-45, from _You Learn by Living_ (HarperCollins)

"Facing it, always facing it, that's the way to get through. Face it."

— Joseph Conrad, writer, from _Typhoon_ (Simon & Schuster)

"I learned that courage was not the absence of fear, but the triumph over it. The brave man is not he who does not feel afraid, but he who conquers that fear."

— Nelson Mandela, anti-apartheid activist and President of South Africa, 1994-99, (Mandela documentary, 1994)

Making your fear your friend

The very idea of facing your fear can, in and of itself, trigger additional fear. However, when you recognize that the purpose of fear is to protect you, uncovering the underlying cause of your fear provides you with the knowledge and understanding that you need to work with your fear, rather than against it.

Do This

Imagine sitting across the table from your Fear. What form does your Fear take? Is it human, animal, or some other kind of creature? Is it tall or short, thin or wide, dark or light? Does it have a gender? Imagining fear this way reveals how you perceive your Fear and also provides a character with which to have a conversation.

Imagine now that you each have a cup of coffee or tea in hand, and you're ready to talk to each other.

For all of the imagined conversation in this activity, write down whatever answers or words first pop into your mind. You can trust your subconscious intuition to supply the voice for your personified fear and, most often, the answers and responses you need will be in the first words that come to mind.

1. **Ask your Fear, "What's your name?"**

Write down the name as it comes to you. That can even be "no name."

_____

2. **Interview your Fear, writing down both your interview questions and Fear's answers.**

Ask questions such as, "Where were you born?" and "Why are you here now?" Allow the conversation to flow, depending on the answers you receive.

_____

_____

_____

_____

_____

_____

_____

_____

_____

_____

_____

3. **Ask your Fear what it's trying to tell you.**

_____

_____

_____

_____

_____

_____

_____

4. **Tell your Fear how you feel about it.**

Be as open and honest as you can, and let your Fear know how it's affecting and/or limiting you.

_____

_____

_____

_____

_____

_____

_____

5. **Ask your Fear if it would be willing to support you in moving forward in your journaling practice.**

If your Fear answers yes, you can discuss the kind of support you want and need. If Fear answers no, ask what your Fear needs in order to support you.

Continue writing the dialogue as needed, until you feel you've come to a resolution of some kind.

_____

_____

_____

_____

_____

_____

_____

_____

_____

6. **Write down what you've discovered about yourself and your obstacles to journaling from your dialogue with Fear.**

For example, perhaps you realized that your Fear was born from a past traumatic event in order to protect you, and that now that you know this, you can calm your fear when it presents itself.

_____

_____

_____

_____

Putting Your Seat in the Seat

Your 15-minute journaling reminder pops up. Suddenly, that report your boss asked for yesterday takes on a strange new urgency. Or you just have to mow the lawn, wash the dishes, or do laundry before you can concentrate on writing. These impulses fall into the category of writing procrastination. And yes, that's a real thing.

In the introduction to his book, *The War of Art*, Steven Pressfield (Black Irish Entertainment, LLC, 2012) writes: "There's a secret that real writers know that wannabe writers don't, and the secret is this: It's not the writing part that's hard. What's hard is sitting down to write. What keeps us from sitting down is resistance."

The point Pressfield makes about resistance causing procrastination applies to journaling as much as it does writing fiction, watercolor painting, learning to dance, or any other endeavor for growth and self-expression.

Avoiding procrastination

Everyone experiences resistance, especially when starting something new or doing anything that takes them out of their comfort zone — even when it's something they really *want* to do.

TIP

Overcome resistance — which usually presents as the urge to procrastinate — by following these steps:

1. **As soon as your alert pops up, remind yourself how good you'll feel after you journal.**

2. **Remind yourself of the reward you plan to give yourself when you finish journaling.**

   Make this reward some type of paired pleasurable activity.

3. **Immediately wrap up whatever you're doing when the alert pops up and go to your journaling space.**

   You should already have set up a dedicated place with your writing supplies (see Chapter 3 for help establishing your journaling space).

4. **Open your journal and begin.**

Center yourself in the moment by closing your eyes and taking a few deep, slow breaths. This will help you slow down and focus on your journaling topic.

Turning off social media and other distractions

Shut down any social media apps, e-mail, and any other potential distractions at the start of your journaling time. How you disconnect depends on how you journal:

>> **By hand:** Turn off your phone and leave it in another room.

>> **Using your phone or computer:** Close e-mail, browser or social media applications, and silence notifications.

Using tools to help you focus

If you have a difficult time avoiding distraction when journaling and you journal on your computer, consider downloading one of the many applications designed to help you focus by automatically blocking access to the Internet and/or social media sites.

Do a web search for *apps for focus and concentration* to find the latest options. Many of these applications are free or have free trials.

Setting the Mood

In addition to the many benefits journaling offers, such as increased sense of well-being and enhanced self-awareness (see Chapter 2 for an in-depth look at journaling's benefits), most people find journaling to be a pleasurable and calming activity. You can enhance the pleasure of journaling (which may also help overcome any initial resistance) by adding a few personal touches. Read on!

Creating a ritual

Make your journaling time a comforting and motivating ritual, as well as an extra special gift to yourself. Choose one or two of the following suggestions to incorporate ritual into your writing time and try them the next time you sit down to journal:

>> Surround yourself with soft pillows.

>> Use soft lighting or natural light.

>> Light a fragrant candle that you use only when you're journaling.

>> Turn on some soft, instrumental music.

>> Have a cup of coffee or tea by your side.

>> Use a special pen or pencil that feels good in your hand.

>> Get cozy with a soft throw or lap blanket.

Breathing deeply and going within

No matter what type of journaling you plan to engage in, take a moment to breathe deeply, bring yourself into the present moment, and feel gratitude for this special gift you're giving yourself.

Breathing deeply and bringing your awareness to where you are in this moment can help you get in touch with your thoughts, emotions, and inner wisdom.

Writing Your Plan

Having a solid plan can help you successfully establish your journaling practice.

Do This

Fill out the following form to create your journaling plan. In the beginning, refer to this plan each week to refresh your motivation. If practical, photocopy or take a picture of your plan, and place it in a prominent location to support your new journaling routine, until it has become a regular part of your life.

Frequency (how often you plan to write):

_____

Time of day or activity paired with:

_____

Added to calendar: ❑

How you hold yourself accountable:

_____

_____

_____

Boundaries you set with others, if applicable:

_____

_____

_____

Methods you use to avoid procrastination and distractions:

_____

_____

_____

How you set the mood for writing:

_____

_____

_____

Exploring Popular Journaling Techniques

IN THIS PART . . .

Use reflective journaling to process and find meaning in life events.

Create calm and tap into your inner wisdom by practicing mindful journaling.

Discover how to organize and manage your life and work by using Bullet Journaling.

Use creative expression techniques to deepen your journaling practice.

Improve your sense of well-being and quality of life by embracing gratitude journaling.

Chapter **5**

Journaling for Reflection

eflective journaling is a structured approach to journaling that focuses on finding meaning in life events by asking questions such as "What happened?" "How did I respond?" and "How did this event change me?"

Through the reflective journaling process, you can examine your thoughts, interpretations, and belief systems to become more self-aware and to grow from your life experiences. In addition, the reflective writing practice can improve your ability to challenge assumptions and think creatively.

Exploring Life with Reflective Journaling

When you picture yourself journaling, you likely see yourself writing in a free-form fashion about thoughts, feelings, and whatever comes to mind. This unstructured technique, referred to as *free-writing*, is probably the most well-known of all journaling methods. (For more information about unstructured journaling, refer to Chapter 1.)

People usually free-write without a specific purpose. Similar to going on a Sunday afternoon drive without having a destination, you're just out to see the sights, and maybe you meander down some side roads on a whim. Your drive may be a fun and relaxing activity that provides perspective on your neighborhood and its surroundings, and might possibly lead to somewhere new and exciting, but that's not the intention. Like that Sunday drive, free-writing may lead to meaningful self-discoveries, but is most often just an exploration of familiar inner roads.

On the other hand, reflective journaling combines intention with exploration. This type of journaling goes on that metaphorical Sunday drive with a final destination in mind. You can still explore interesting sights and meander down those side roads along the way, but you arrive at a meaningful destination. Your trip fulfills a purpose beyond just getting in the car and driving.

REMEMBER

Reflective journaling is a therapeutic practice that can help you identify, grow from, and find meaning in your past experiences. And the new perspective you gain along the way can change the way you respond to people and events in the future.

We create our life stories by making meaning of events that happen in our lives. Reflective journaling allows you to reconsider those stories, to deeply explore all sides of an event, and to confirm or even rewrite those stories. Check out the nearby sidebar for an example.

REMEMBER

You can use reflective journaling to examine events in the distant past, like in my example, or events that happened just yesterday. You can also use it to reflect on important topics in your life: relationships, life passages, parenting, and more.

Fortunately, like most journaling methods, you can quickly get the hang of reflective journaling. And, with practice, you can turn it into a powerful tool to enhance your understanding of your past, increase self-knowledge and self-awareness, help you change how you respond in stressful situations, and even improve relationships.

HOW REFLECTIVE JOURNALING CAN CHANGE A LIFE STORY

When I was writing my first memoir, I used reflective journaling as a tool to deepen my understanding of my family dynamics. When I was growing up, I had five brothers and was the only girl. My brothers were the rough and tumble variety, quite wild at times, and could be cruel to one another and to me. In my memory, it seemed we were always fighting and beating each other up.

Yet, when I began using reflective writing techniques to examine my memories, I realized that, compared with how my brothers treated each other, they had gone easy on me. Really only one brother occasionally hit me. That realization enabled me to rewrite my internal family story. I was no longer the victim of mean brothers; instead, I was finally able to acknowledge that I had been privileged as the only girl and treated more kindly than they treated one another. Quite a revelation!

Defining reflection

Before you dive into practicing reflective journaling, I want to make sure you understand what I mean when I say "reflection."

You can interpret the term *reflection* in a number of ways that apply to your reflective journaling practice. *To reflect* may include any or all of the following:

>> **To cause to change direction:** "The glass reflects the light." Reflective journaling can *reflect light on,* or bring insight to, related concepts, issues, and behaviors. For example, while reflecting on your relationship with your son, you suddenly see a similarity in your relationship with your father. Your reflective thinking bounces the light off the surface of your intended subject (your son) to a nearby subject (your father), which ultimately provides some insight into yourself in the process.

>> **To mirror back:** "The still water of the lake reflects the trees along its banks." Nothing provides self-awareness as effectively as a mirror. Reflective journaling gives you the

opportunity to see your behaviors and attitudes mirrored back to you, simply through the act of writing about them as well as reading and analyzing your entries afterwards. And when you maintain an intention of remaining curious about yourself, you can use reflective journaling to understand yourself better and make purposeful change in your life.

» **To make apparent:** "Their work reflects their attitude." You may have difficulty seeing patterns in your own life. However, writing consistently about the same issues from different angles can provide a work of reflection. Much like weaving a blanket thread by thread, then stepping back to see the patterns you created, reviewing journaling entries made over time can help you perceive behavioral patterns in your life.

» **To consider or think carefully about:** "They reflected on the many mistakes they had made." This definition provides the most direct explanation of what you're doing when you write reflectively in your journal. You simply write down the thoughts, emotions, and responses that you have while you consider your topic.

Seeing the benefits of reflection

Simply thinking or writing about your past doesn't necessarily involve true reflection.

WARNING

Don't play past events in your head over and over again, a practice called *ruminating*. This process doesn't provide any constructive insights and can actually be unhealthy. Ruminating about your past can lead you to beat yourself up mentally about past mistakes and to dwell on regrets. Looking back in this manner can lead to sadness, anger, and depression.

In contrast, reflective journaling, done with intention and purpose, provides a constructive outlet. You can get many benefits from considering past events introspectively and, in particular, thinking about your responses to those events. Here are a few potential benefits of reflective journaling. Reflection can

» **Help you make connections between experiences.**
These connections, in turn, help you to see the past from a
new perspective. Looking back, you can express compassion and empathy to that past version of yourself and
other people who played a role in hurtful events in
your life.

For example, a good friend did something that seemed like
an intentional slight at the time. Upon reflection, you can
now perceive their behavior for what it was: They had a lot
going on in their life, felt overwhelmed, and couldn't give
you what you needed. They didn't slight you intentionally,
you now realize. This realization, then, opens the door to
forgiveness and healing.

» **Improve your critical thinking skills.** One of the purposes of reflective journaling is to question assumptions
you make about people and events in your life. An
assumption is an unexamined belief or way of thinking that
you've taken for granted. Assumptions guide conclusions
and decisions you make, so becoming aware of and
questioning your assumptions is key to critical thinking,
resulting in improved self-awareness and better decision
making.

» **Show you how far you've come.** Each day, you do the
best you can, but you can't easily tell if you improve much
over time. When you reflect on past behaviors and
relationships, and compare those behaviors and relationships with where you are today, you can see how much
you've changed and grown. And if you realize that you
haven't changed much, that realization can spur you to
make life course corrections.

» **Give you the opportunity to reassess what you want in
your life.** Reflecting on where you've been and what you've
experienced allows you to decide what you like or want in
your life and what you don't. It can inspire you to recommit
to goals or change direction altogether.

Getting Started with Reflective Journaling

The best way to figure out how to do something is to do it. So, grab a pen (or pencil) and a timer (you can use the timer on your smartphone, if you have one) and get ready to try a short reflective writing exercise that I outline in the following sections.

Step 1: Focusing on your purpose

What do you want to better understand or discover more about? Perhaps something happened this week at work or at home that you want to consider. Maybe you had an argument with a loved one, and you want to think more clearly about the dynamics involved in that interaction. Or you want to gain additional perspective about an event that occurred in your childhood.

You can choose any topic, whether you consider it negative or positive, to explore in your writing. To start, I recommend choosing a topic that evokes some emotional response in you — but avoid events or topics that involve trauma or that you find particularly painful.

Whatever the topic or event, approach it with genuine curiosity and a desire to find out more about yourself in the process of writing about it.

Before you begin each journaling session, write down the purpose for that session. For example: *I want to understand more about what happened yesterday when John and I argued over who would clean the kitchen.*

Do This

Write down the purpose for your reflection today:

_____

_____

_____

Step 2: Setting a time limit

You don't have to set a time limit, but I highly recommend it — especially when you're beginning your reflective journaling practice. Here are my top five reasons for limiting your writing time. Setting a time limit

» **Makes sitting down to write feel less overwhelming.** When you first start out, developing a journal writing practice can feel like a huge time commitment. You may find you have less desire to procrastinate if you know you're committing only 10 or 20 minutes, tops.

» **Gives you a goal to shoot for.** If you don't yet write regularly, achieving the significant goal of writing continuously for even five minutes provides positive reinforcement.

» **Leaves you hungry for more.** When the timer goes off, complete whatever sentence or thought you're in the middle of. If you didn't finish your reflection on that particular event or topic — perhaps something came up in today's writing that you want to explore more deeply — you already know what to write about during your next journaling session.

» **Helps you focus.** When you know you have a limited amount of time in which to write, you naturally concentrate more during that time.

» **Gets you in the habit.** You can more easily create a journaling habit when you dedicate a small amount of time to practicing it on a regular basis, rather than writing for long periods of time less frequently.

Do This

Set a timer for the number of minutes you want to journal, but don't start it just yet. First, figure out the questions that you want to ask yourself to increase the benefits of reflection. The following section explains why and how to structure your journaling.

Step 3: Structuring your writing process

Although you could just start free-writing about your topic without any specific prompts, having a structure can help you get started faster, give you a different perspective on what happened, and dig deeper to uncover underlying causes or issues that you might not be aware of before journaling.

REMEMBER

Structure gives you a framework upon which to build your understanding and increase your insights and take-aways from your journaling.

The following sections present my two favorite methods to begin my own reflective writing explorations.

Using the 5Ws+1H

One of the easiest — and most effective — ways to begin reflecting on a past event involves using the 5Ws of good journalism (which you probably remember from school) — Who, What, When, Where, and Why — plus How.

TIP

When answering the W questions (plus H), write down whatever first comes to mind and don't worry about whether it's "right" or accurate. Accuracy doesn't matter — you want to explore your thoughts and emotions on the subject.

Here's an example:

Jody wants to reflect on an interaction she had with one of her employees, which left her feeling awkward and confused. She wants to understand what happened so that she can improve her relationship with that employee and avoid that kind of awkwardness in the future.

After she writes her intention at the top of her journal page, she starts her timer and begins writing about the situation using the 5Ws+1H:

> **Who was involved?** *My employee, Susan, and me.*
>
> **What happened?** *We were discussing ideas for her next project, when she suddenly became quiet and seemed distracted.*

I attempted to reengage her on the topic, but she just seemed like she wanted to be anywhere else. So I ended our meeting early.

When did it happen? *During our weekly one-on-one. It was mid-morning on a busy Wednesday.*

Where was I (both physically and in my life) at the time? *We were meeting online via Zoom. I was having a busy morning and was really focused on getting something accomplished during our meeting. I was also stressing about the presentation I would be giving to our executive team that afternoon.*

Why do I think Susan and I responded the way we did? *I'm not sure. Maybe she truly was simply distracted by something that happened in her home while we were talking. Or maybe something I said upset her. Admittedly, I was super focused on defining how we were going to move forward with the project, and I was throwing out a lot of ideas. Maybe I wasn't letting her speak enough or she felt I was rejecting her ideas.*

Why did I end the meeting early? *I felt unsure of myself and didn't know how to proceed. It just seemed easier to end the meeting and try again later.*

How can I change my response in the future? *In the future, instead of avoiding confronting the issue, I think I should simply say what I'm observing and ask Susan if she's distracted and why. If she's hesitant to answer, I'll invite her to let me know when I need to give her more space to express her ideas. I can make a commitment to speak less and be a better listener.*

Do This

Think about the purpose you wrote down previously for your journaling session (see the section "Step 1: Focusing on your purpose"). Start your timer (from "Step 2: Setting a time limit") and answer the following questions.

Who was involved?

_____

_____

_____

What happened? (Be as detailed as possible in your description.)

_____

_____

_____

_____

_____

_____

_____

_____

When did it happen? (Include not just date and time, but where you were in your day or life, emotionally.)

_____

_____

_____

_____

_____

How did this happen? What were some of the underlying issues or causes?

_____

_____

_____

_____

_____

_____

What can I learn from this situation/event?

_____

_____

_____

_____

_____

How can I change my response to similar situations in the future?

_____

_____

_____

_____

_____

You aren't limited to these exact questions when using the 5Ws+1H technique in future journaling sessions. You can use any Who, What, When, Where, Why, and How questions that are relevant to your topic.

Applying the "what I mean by" prompt

What if, rather than reflecting on a single event or a series of events in your life, you simply want to explore an issue, question, or decision you need to make?

Using the "what I mean by" prompt structure can help you dig deeper and get more out of your writing.

Just follow these simple but effective steps:

1. **Write your purpose at the top of your journal entry.**

2. **Set your timer and start it.**

3. **Start writing about your topic.**

4. **After you write a sentence or two, select a key word or phrase from what you wrote.**

   Choose any word or phrase from your writing that catches your attention or stands out for you.

5. **Start the next sentence with "What I mean by [insert your word or phrase] is . . ."**

Let me share an example from one of my own journal entries. I was in the process of writing down my goals and began to question why I performed this ritual on the first of January each year. Why not some other day? Here's what I wrote, using the "what I mean by" prompt, to dig deeper into my motivations and understand myself better:

> *January 1st always feels momentous, as though it is a fresh start to something new. . . . A new year invites new awareness, new thinking, newness of all kinds.* ***What I mean by "new"*** *is fresh, without attachment to what has already been done, seen, felt, thought, or heard. New means untouched in some way, unused. A new shirt has never been worn, never washed, the colors are still fresh and bright. It fits well and looks good. New thinking is like that. Fresh, bright perspective, unused, fits well for the situation or the day. Newness also embodies hope. With hope, we are always looking forward. The same is true of new. Worn represents the past. Review, reflect, re . . . always looks to the past. Making, creating, thinking, being, these things are present. New begins now and looks forward.*

I went on to explore what I meant by the words *perspective* and *hope.* In the end, I gained some valuable insights about myself.

TIP

As an alternative way to use this prompt, turn it into a question: "What do I mean by [insert word or phrase]?"

Do This

Thinking about the purpose for your journaling session, start your timer and begin writing. Stop after the second sentence, select any word or phrase from what you wrote, and continue with the "what I mean by" prompt.

_____

_____

_____

_____

_____

_____

_____

_____

_____

_____

_____

_____

Step 4: Reflecting on the writing process

To get the most from your structured journaling time, at the end of each writing session, review your purpose and then reflect on what you discovered in the writing process. This "review and reflect" process should only take two to five minutes to complete.

Do This

Review the purpose you wrote down at the beginning of your last journaling session. How do you feel about what you wrote, and did you gain the insight you wanted? Use the space provided to write your response.

_____

_____

_____

_____

_____

Writing Through Time

Reflective journaling is effective for more than just writing about your past. Writing reflectively is like holding your life up to·a magic mirror so that you can see it more clearly. Moreover, this mirror doesn't depend on time. It enables you to see into the past, present, and future.

Of course, you need practice to accomplish this bit of time-traveling magic. The more you use this time-travel mirror, the more you become aware of patterns in your life, which allows you to delve deeper into what makes you tick, increasing self-awareness and understanding.

Shining a light on the past

If you're like most people, you probably cycle stories about your past — especially traumatic or hurtful events and mistakes that you've made — over and over again in your mind. Whatever happened in the past has no control over your future, but how you perceive the past often dictates how you respond to what happens today. When you continue to identify with the "you" of your past, you continue to move in the same direction.

Using reflective journaling to write about past events can help you shift in a more positive direction. You can transform those painful stories into healing stories, destructive thoughts into constructive thoughts, and confusion into clarity — freeing you to decide how you want to respond based on who you want to be, rather than responding reflexively based on who you thought you were.

REMEMBER

To use reflective journaling effectively, you need to shine a light on the events of your past and consider those events and your interpretation of those events anew. Simply expressing emotions during your journaling — whether you're talking or writing about them — doesn't always provide you with new insights. To tap into the power of journaling, you need to question your previous perceptions and use your writing to gain insight into and make changes based on your past — maybe even revising your internalized story around those events.

Do This

In this exercise, you combine the 5Ws+1H questions (Who, What, When, Where, Why, and How) with the "what I mean by" prompt (from the "Applying the 'what I mean by' prompt" section earlier in this chapter).

Think of an event in your past or a time in your life that you want to explore — a situation that you want to understand better. Maybe something happened that has always bothered you, and you want to understand why you felt so strongly about it. Or maybe you want to explore an accomplishment you feel proud of to figure out what you did right and how you can repeat that success in future endeavors. Whatever you choose, thinking about it should evoke some emotion in you.

WARNING

Until you have more practice with this method, don't select a traumatic event or occurrence that causes overwhelming emotions. I discuss how to approach healing from trauma in Chapter 10.

Write a brief title for your event.

_____

_____

_____

Write your purpose for exploring the event. In other words, what do you hope to get out of writing about it?

_____

_____

_____

_____

_____

_____

Set a timer for the number of minutes you want to journal and write to the following questions and statements.

REMEMBER

If the timer goes off before you complete the prompts, simply finish your thought, and then leave the rest of the questions for your next writing session. Take your time and journal thoughtfully. Don't feel rushed to complete all the prompts in one sitting.

Describe the situation. What, when, and where did it happen?

_____

_____

_____

_____

_____

_____

Besides you, who else was involved?

_____

_____

_____

How did you feel and respond at the time?

_____

_____

_____

_____

_____

How has it affected your life?

_____

_____

_____

_____

_____

Select a key word or phrase from your previous answer and complete the sentence, "What I mean by [insert key word or phrase] is . . ."

_____

_____

_____

_____

_____

What have I discovered about myself since that event that can help me see others or myself differently?

_____

_____

_____

_____

_____

_____

Select a key word or phrase from your previous answer and complete the sentence, "What I mean by [insert key word or phrase] is . . ."

_____

_____

_____

_____

_____

If that same situation were to occur today, I would . . .

_____

_____

_____

_____

_____

_____

How does my anticipated response today differ from my original response? How have I grown or become a stronger person since then?

_____

_____

_____

_____

_____

If I could go back in time and give my younger self advice, I would say . . .

_____

_____

_____

_____

_____

Wrap up your session by reviewing and reflecting on what you wrote. Read back through everything you wrote, circling any words or phrases that stand out to you. (This circling process can help you identify recurring themes and patterns in your thinking and behaviors.) What has the writing process shown you and how has it helped you change your story about yourself?

_____

_____

_____

_____

_____

_____

Contemplating change in the present

When you journal about your present life, you most often find yourself writing about changes you're experiencing — disruptions to jobs, relationships, children, housing, health, or broader world events. Reflecting on how you react to these changes helps you see how to take control of your thoughts and emotions — and, ultimately, how you respond to change in general.

REMEMBER

Change means making decisions. Reflective journaling can help you gain clarity on what you truly need and want, as well as weigh the pros and cons of various paths, assisting you in your decision-making process.

Change is inevitable, as much a part of living as the weather. Yet, for many people, even the very word *change* evokes strong emotions, ranging from dread to excitement. When you think about change, where on this spectrum do your emotions fall? Do you tend to resist, embrace, or simply roll with change?

If you tend to resist change, rest assured that you're not alone in responding that way. In fact, the vast majority of people's first emotional reaction to change involves a feeling of resistance. And no wonder. Change can be unnerving, especially when an event or decision outside of your control brings it on. Change means loss, while also opening doors to new opportunities. Even change that you initiated and believe in brings stress, challenges, and the need to adapt to new ways of doing things. Change can push you way outside your comfort zone, forcing you to gain new skills and adopt new approaches to the way you live or work.

Perhaps the most unsettling thing about change is not knowing exactly where you'll end up. What will happen in the future? Navigating change can feel like you're driving at high speed through a thick fog, only able to see a few feet of road ahead of you at any time. But change also brings opportunities for creativity and growth.

Whether you associate change with dread or excitement, reflective journaling can help you identify and analyze your deep-seated responses to change, as well as create ways to successfully cope with it. Writing reflectively about the change you experience can decrease stress. It can also help you shift your thoughts — which, in turn, shifts your feelings toward a more optimistic outcome.

Exploring your responses and feelings about change can help you take control of your thoughts and attitudes, helping clear some of that metaphorical fog so that you see more clearly where you're going.

Do This

In this exercise, you use the 5Ws+1H idea to explore change (see the "Using the 5Ws+1H" section for more info). Start by thinking of a change, small or large, you are currently experiencing or are considering. Maybe you're going through a home remodel. Or maybe you're planning to go back to school or change careers. Whatever you choose, thinking about this change should evoke some emotion in you.

Create a brief title for your journal entry (what change are you writing about?):

_____

_____

_____

What is your purpose for writing about this change?

_____

_____

_____

Set a timer for the number of minutes you want to journal, start it, and write to the following questions and statements. If the timer goes off before you complete the prompts, finish your thought, and then leave the rest of the questions for your next writing session.

Briefly describe the change you're facing.

_____

_____

_____

_____

_____

_____

Who or what initiated the change, and who else does it affect?

_____

_____

_____

_____

_____

_____

Where were you when you made the decision to initiate this change or when you first realized the change was occurring?

_____

_____

_____

What was your first reaction, and where in your body did you feel your emotion?

_____

_____

_____

_____

_____

_____

What might you lose as a result of this change?

_____

_____

_____

_____

_____

_____

What opportunities exist, and what could you gain from the change? Write down all the positive things that could happen as a result.

_____

_____

_____

_____

_____

_____

Brainstorm a list of actions that you can take to help you cope with and gain the most from this new direction.

_____

_____

_____

_____

_____

Wrap up your session by reviewing and reflecting on what you wrote. Read back through everything you wrote, circling any words or phrases that stand out to you in order to reveal repeating images, themes, and thought patterns.

How have your feelings about the change shifted?

_____

_____

_____

_____

_____

_____

What have you discovered about yourself through the writing process?

_____

_____

_____

_____

_____

Considering the future

Your reflective-writing magic mirror can't act as a crystal ball. You can't use it to foretell the future, but you can use it to *envision* the future that you want and determine what you need to do to accomplish that desired life.

In addition to reflecting on past experiences and processing current challenges in your life, reflective journaling can help you envision a positive future for yourself, identify goals that you want to reach, and determine the actions that you need to take to get there.

Although unstructured thinking about the future can cause some anxiety, especially when the world around you is in turmoil, considering your future with creativity and optimism can improve psychological well-being and make your life feel more meaningful.

When you write down your dreams, intentions, and goals for the future — whether you write about your next vacation or your dream home — you are, in a very real sense, writing your future into being. You are more likely to achieve what you want when you write it down or create a visual representation, such as a vision board. (A *vision board* is a collage, usually made on poster-board, containing images and words to visualize the things you desire.) These written and visual representations of your intention work because they increase your internal identification with the future self you're creating.

Do This

In this exercise, use the 5Ws+1H to envision the future (see "Using the 5Ws+1H" earlier in this chapter). Start by thinking about what you want your life to be like in the near or the far future (either one works). Maybe you hope to buy a home, find your dream job, discover love, or go on an epic adventure. Whatever you dream, thinking about it should provide a sense of pleasure and hope.

Create a title for your journal entry. What dream(s) are you writing about?

_____

_____

_____

What's your purpose for journaling today? What about your future dreams do you want to explore through writing?

_____

_____

_____

_____

_____

_____

Set a timer for the number of minutes you want to journal and write to the following questions and statements. When you're reflecting on the future, you most likely need more than one session to fully explore your subject, especially if you've never done this before.

TIP

For best results, give yourself time to fully visualize your dream(s) while writing. When the timer goes off, finish your thoughts on the current prompt, and then come back to complete the remaining prompts in your next writing session.

What do you want to have more of in your life?

_____

_____

_____

_____

_____

Who do you want to become?

_____

_____

_____

_____

_____

With whom do you want to build better/stronger relationships?

_____

_____

_____

_____

_____

_____

What do you want to know more about?

_____

_____

_____

_____

_____

What does your ideal day look like? Describe this day in detail, starting with waking in the morning and ending with going to bed at night.

_____

_____

_____

_____

_____

_____

_____

_____

When do you see yourself living your desired life? Do you see it happening in the near or distant future, or can you achieve some of it now and some later? Spend a few minutes reflecting on your desires (what you want) and the challenges to getting there.

_____

_____

_____

_____

_____

_____

Brainstorm a list of 10 doable actions that answer this question: How can you get more of what you want in your life, build those better relationships, and achieve that ideal day? These actions can include taking a class, getting up earlier (or later), starting a new habit, or even exploring a new career.

REMEMBER

Keep in mind that you're brainstorming. Don't censor yourself. No idea is a bad idea, and just because you write it here doesn't mean you have to do it. You simply want to generate a list of actions that might help you live the life you want.

List all the actions you can think of here:

1. _____

2. _____

3. _____

4. _____

5. _____

6. _____

7. _____

8. _____

9. _____

10. _____

After brainstorming, take time to review and reflect on what you wrote. How do you feel after writing about your dreams and ways to achieve them?

_____

_____

_____

_____

_____

_____

Deepening Reflection to Uncover Gold

Although you can figure out the basics of reflective journaling easily, how to reflect *deeply* comes only with practice. If you want to uncover more about your hidden motivations and desires — in other words, if you want to find out more about yourself — you need to figure out how to dig deeper into the stories you tell yourself.

TIP

If, after journaling, you don't feel like you've discovered anything new about yourself, others, or the situation, and you still feel unresolved or have intense or mixed feelings, then you haven't gone deep enough. Significant life events and topics may require an extended period of time — a week or more — of regular reflective journaling to get to the bottom of them.

Whatever your journaling purpose — whether you want to make sense of your past, cope with current situations, or envision your future — you likely need to spend more than one writing session on that topic in order to fully understand it and how it affects your thoughts, emotions, and decision-making process.

After all, it took a lifetime of experiences and responses to form your internal stories, which in turn inform your thoughts, feelings, and attitudes. It only stands to reason that it also takes time to fully comprehend the path you took to get where you are.

Knowledge is power, and self-knowledge is empowerment. The following sections discuss two of my favorite methods for diving deeper into self-understanding and gaining inner strength.

Writing more with a daily twist

In this straightforward method, simply continue to write daily (or at your set regular intervals) on the same topic. For each session, record your title and purpose for writing that day. Add a slight twist by varying your purpose each time. A different purpose enables you to pursue new thoughts and emotional directions by using the 5Ws+1H (Who, What, When, Where, Why, and How) technique.

For example, if your original purpose was, "I want to understand why my uncle acts the way he does at family events," you might follow up with a variation, such as, "I want to understand why my uncle's behavior bothers me so much."

Create your own Who, What, When, Where, Why, and How questions as appropriate for your topic, similar to the 5W+1H prompts shown previously in this chapter. Then respond to those questions in your journal.

Focus on the What and How questions for the deepest insights. For example, "*What* is it about my uncle's behavior that irritates me?" encourages a more detailed reply than "*Why* does my uncle's behavior irritate me?" In the same way, "*How* does his behavior affect me?" can bring forth a more introspective answer than "*Why* does his behavior affect me?"

Mining past entries

Another time-tested method for deepening your reflective writing practice involves spending a few minutes scanning what you wrote in previous entries. Look for repetitive phrases, patterns, or insights (those aha moments). Keep a set of highlighters or colored pens on hand to highlight or circle these key words and phrases so that you can see them at a glance. They can reveal themes and thoughts or behavioral patterns in your life.

After reviewing your entries in this way, write about any new insights you discover about yourself (or anything or anyone else) during the reading.

TIP

Do this journal-history scanning session as a separate journaling session, not immediately following one. Just as you can see more of a landscape vista from a distance, you can see more key phrases and patterns when you get a little distance from your previous writing, even if only for a day or two.

As I discuss in the section "Step 1: Focusing on your purpose," earlier in this chapter, title your entry and state your purpose. For consistency in your journaling practice, you can set a timer and/or split this review into multiple sessions, but I recommend allowing extra time for this activity if you have a lot of entries to review and you enjoy uninterrupted contemplation.

When you finish scanning and highlighting your entries, ask yourself the following questions:

>> What do the repetitive words and phrases tell me?

>> Do I see any constructive or destructive patterns?

>> What story am I creating about myself?

>> How does this story help me?

>> If I wanted to change this story to help me more, how would I change it?

Make notes in the margins while you consider these questions and jot down any additional ideas and thoughts that occur to you. If you want, free-write about the journal review experience and what you gained from it. (I talk about free-writing in Chapter 1 and again briefly in the "Exploring Life with Reflective Journaling" section at the beginning of this chapter.)

IN THIS CHAPTER

» **Exploring what it means to be mindful**

» **Putting yourself in the present moment**

» **Connecting mindfulness and awareness**

» **Preparing to write by focusing your awareness**

» **Practicing mindful journaling**

Chapter **6**

Focusing on the Present: Mindful Journaling

Journaling can help you feel more centered and improve your sense of inner peace.

Mindful journaling is similar to reflective journaling (which you can read about in Chapter 5) in that you use it to examine your thoughts and feelings and raise self-awareness. However, you don't use mindful journaling to process past events or future plans. Rather, it's a meditative writing process that tunes into your current thoughts and feelings and releases them into your journal.

In this chapter, I discuss how mindful journaling works and share ways to combine mindfulness exercises with journaling.

Reaping the Benefits of Mindful Journaling

Combining simple mindfulness practices — such as meditation — with journaling, helps you center yourself in the present moment. And when you're fully present, you can freely explore in writing what you're feeling while letting go of self-judgment and self-doubt. Writing mindfully leads quite naturally to increased self-compassion and self-understanding, as well as bringing clarity to your thinking and decision-making.

HOW MINDFULNESS CAME TO THE WEST

The concept of mindfulness came to the Western world in the 1970s through the work of scientist, writer, and meditation teacher, Jon Kabat-Zinn, Ph.D. Kabat-Zinn had studied Buddhism under Philip Kapleau (a Zen missionary) and Thich Nhat Hanh (a renowned Vietnamese monk), among others. Later, he adapted the Buddhist teachings on mindfulness, integrating their concepts with scientific principles, and founded the Stress Reduction Clinic in 1979 at the University of Massachusetts Medical School.

In 1990, Kabat-Zinn's ideas gained national notice when his first book, *Full Catastrophe Living: Using the Wisdom of Your Body and Mind to Face Stress, Pain, and Illness*, was published by Random House Publishing Group and subsequently featured on PBS.

Since then, mindfulness meditation and other mindfulness practices, such as mindful journaling, have become mainstream in Western culture and a lifestyle for many thousands of people.

Now, healthcare, medicine, schools, professional sports, and even the legal profession utilize mindfulness practices because the effects have been shown to reduce stress, anxiety, and pain, as well as enhance physical health and healing processes.

Mindful journaling is part of one of the fastest growing health-care trends in the U.S. in recent years, along with practices such as meditation, yoga, and play-inspired activities.

Mindful journaling has become popular for many reasons:

>> Reduces stress by quieting the amygdala, that "fight or flight" part of the brain

>> Improves concentration and focus

>> Shifts negative thinking to a positive point of view

>> Nurtures compassion for self and others

>> Increases self-acceptance

Centering Yourself: The Importance of Being Present

Centering yourself in the present moment is at the heart of mindful journaling. The present moment is a place without time. It is only now . . . and now . . . and now. It's impossible for anything to actually exist outside of the present moment because everything in the past and the future is a construct of your mind. They don't exist in the now, only in your imagination.

Worry and stress are produced by anticipating the future. Emotional pain is produced and carried forward within by focusing on something that happened in the past. So you can greatly reduce — if not eliminate altogether — stress, worry, and emotional pain by figuring out how to bring your attention to the now, refer to the past only when it's relevant to the present moment, and not anticipate the future.

Such is the power of mindfulness.

REMEMBER

To be in the present is to ask yourself, "What's going on around and inside me at this moment?" And then sit quietly and observe the answers to your question. Anytime you begin to analyze or judge your thoughts, your attention shifts away from the present moment.

When you focus on what's going on around and inside you right now — exactly now — you may notice several things happening in your mind and body, including increased awareness of sensory information, such as sounds and smells; physical sensations; and the thoughts and feelings resulting from what you're noticing.

You may experience other sensations or find that you occasionally get distracted, and that's okay, too. Remember not to judge yourself, because whatever you are and whatever you're noticing in the moment isn't right or wrong — it just *is*.

Exploring Mindfulness and How to Become More Aware

In order to successfully use mindful journaling techniques, it's important to first clarify your understanding of what it means to be *mindful*. The following sections help you do just that, as well as tune into your thoughts, emotions, and physical sensations.

Determining what mindfulness means to you

The experience and understanding of mindfulness (being present) can mean different things to different people. Before beginning your mindful journaling exploration, take the time to define what mindfulness means to *you*. Your definition (which may change over time) guides your expectations for what you want to gain from mindful journaling.

Do This

To identify what mindfulness means to you, answer the following questions in the space provided.

What mindfulness practices, if any, have you done in the past or do you do regularly now?

_____

_____

_____

_____

What makes those practices mindful, and how did (or do) you feel when engaged in them?

_____

_____

_____

_____

Complete the following sentence: "For me, being in a mindful state means . . ."

_____

_____

_____

_____

The Merriam-Webster dictionary defines *mindfulness* as "the practice of maintaining a nonjudgmental state of heightened or complete awareness of one's thoughts, emotions, or experiences on a moment-to-moment basis; *also:* such a state of awareness."

Does this definition inspire additional ideas or understanding of mindfulness for you? If so, feel free to add those ideas to what you wrote.

With a better understanding of what mindfulness means to you personally, try the exercises in the following sections to explore how to be present to physical sensations as well as the thoughts and feelings you are experiencing.

Body scanning: Tuning into physical sensations

REMEMBER

One important aspect of mindfulness involves becoming aware of the sensations in your body. Tune into those sensations by taking a *body scan*, which is to slowly and systematically bring your awareness to your physical sensations, from head to toe.

Most of the time, while you go about your day, you probably don't think about your body unless you're uncomfortable in some way and the sensations are calling for your attention: That cut on your finger is throbbing, or you're hungry or thirsty, or you have to go to the bathroom, or something has caused you to feel self-conscious physically. Otherwise, unless your body's demanding notice, you might simply take for granted that it will carry you where you want to go and function like it's supposed to.

Do This

In this exercise, you perform a body scan by slowly moving your attention to the sensations in different parts of your body, from top to bottom, followed by journaling about your body-scan experience. Scanning your body in this way is an effective method for calming and centering yourself in the present moment and preparing for mindful journaling.

Follow these steps:

1. **Find a safe, solitary place where you feel comfortable.**

   Before starting any mindful journaling exercise, make sure that you're in a location where you can be undisturbed and feel safe enough to close your eyes.

2. **Read through all the steps in this list before you begin putting them into practice.**

   By knowing the steps before you begin, you can focus your attention on your practice and not on reading.

3. **Get in a comfortable, relaxed position.**

   You can sit, either on a chair or a floor cushion, or lie down on any comfortable surface, such as a yoga mat or bed.

4. Inhale deeply and, while you exhale, let your eyes close.

5. Focus your attention on the top of your head.

How does your scalp feel? Does it tingle? Can you feel which way your hair falls? What thoughts or emotions come up, if any?

6. Notice these sensations and emotions in a passive way, and then imagine them floating away.

As you proceed through the body-scan steps, don't judge or consciously try to change anything in your body, but do notice (and let it happen) if something changes just because you're looking at it.

7. Next, move your attention to your face.

Feel the muscles around your eyes. Are they tight or relaxed? What about your cheeks and around your mouth? What happens when you focus on each part of your face?

8. Moving down your body, one by one, focus on the sensations in your neck, shoulders, and upper back.

Spend a few moments paying attention to each of these areas. What do you notice? What sensations stand out? What do these sensations tell you?

If you find yourself judging or having negative thoughts about your body, simply notice the thought and release it by imagining it floating away. Then return your attention to the present moment and the part of your body that you're focusing on.

9. Move your focus to your arms, moving slowly from your upper arms to your forearms and then your hands.

Take your time. Notice how you've positioned them, if you move them, and whether they're relaxed or tense. Notice any thoughts and emotions that arise.

10. Continue to your chest, directing your attention there.

While you focus on your chest, notice how it rises and falls with your breathing. Notice if you're breathing deep or shallow, slow or fast.

11. Now, focus on your abdomen.

Do you feel hungry or full? What other sensations do you have here?

12. **Continue on down to your buttocks, then thighs, and then hamstrings.**

Again, just pay attention to the way they feel and any thoughts and emotions that arise. Don't try to change anything.

13. **Focus in turn on your calves, ankles, feet, and toes.**

14. **As you complete your body scan, feel your body as a whole, all the pieces connected.**

What do you notice about this internal image of your body, your overall sensations, thoughts, and feelings?

15. **Finally, open your eyes and write your responses to the following questions.**

Immediately journaling after your body scan helps to extend and add a layer of understanding to your experience of being present with your body.

What stands out for you about scanning your body for sensations?

_____

_____

_____

_____

How did this exercise feel as you were doing it? What thoughts and emotions came up for you?

_____

_____

_____

_____

_____

_____

_____

How do you feel now, in this moment?

_____

_____

_____

_____

Paying attention to your thoughts

In the same way that focusing on your physical sensations (as discussed in the preceding section) centers you in the present moment through your body, journaling while observing your thoughts anchors you to the present and heightens your self-awareness. Paying attention to your thoughts forces your mind to slow down, allowing you to bring the flow of your thoughts into the light of consciousness, where you can choose to linger over them or let them go.

You may have heard the Buddhist term *monkey mind*, which describes the way your restless mind jumps from one thought to the next, like a monkey swinging from one branch to another.

Humans are nothing if not thinking beings. The problem is that our monkey-mind thoughts are constant and difficult to control. In fact, one could argue that they are, in fact, uncontrollable, and trying to have power over thoughts is like trying to dominate the wind.

For example, if I tell you, "Don't think of a purple dinosaur," you'll probably immediately think of a purple dinosaur, whether you want to or not. That's the nature of thought.

Your monkey mind is also your inner critic, the voice in your head that's always telling you what you're doing wrong and why you don't deserve to have good things in your life. It's always worrying about the future, which raises your anxiety level and makes life feel overwhelming.

Although the monkey mind is part of who you are as a human, you don't have to be ruled by it.

Mindfulness meditation is the practice of passively observing thoughts as they arise, without judging or holding onto them. Allowing your thoughts to simply pass through your conscious attention without analyzing or directing them calms the monkey mind.

Mindful journaling builds on mindfulness meditation by further slowing down this observation process, continuing to pay attention to your thoughts without judgment or direction, and allowing them to flow from your mind onto the page of your journal.

Do This

Use the following mindful journaling exercise to consciously tune into your thoughts without attempting to steer them in any particular direction. This method is also known as *stream-of-consciousness writing*. Just follow these steps:

1. **Find a location where you can be undisturbed and feel safe enough to relax.**

2. **Get in a comfortable position in which to write.**

3. **Inhale deeply and, while you exhale, let your eyes close.**

4. **Focus on your breathing.**

   Breathe slowly, counting four beats in and four beats out. Continue counting breaths until you feel relaxed, calm, and fully present.

5. **Open your eyes and write the answer to the question, "What is on my mind in this moment?" in the space provided.**

6. **Then, write the next thought, and the next, and the next, without pausing and without judging what you're writing.**

   Simply allow your thoughts to flow through you and onto the page. It's okay to repeat thoughts, phrases, or sentences. Notice the repetition, and then let it go.

7. **Continue writing until your stream of conscious thoughts subside.**

_____

_____

_____

_____

_____

_____

_____

_____

_____

_____

_____

_____

_____

_____

_____

_____

_____

_____

_____

_____

_____

_____

_____

How did this exercise feel? Were you comfortable with it, or did it feel strange to let your thoughts flow so freely and not hold onto them?

_____

_____

_____

Read what you wrote while journaling. What themes, repeating thoughts, worries, or flights of imagination do you notice, if any? What interests you most about what you wrote? Include your thoughts here.

_____

_____

_____

_____

_____

_____

Centering on the Moment

The exercises in the section "Exploring Mindfulness and How to Become More Aware," earlier in this chapter, can help you become more aware of your body, mind, and emotions while focusing only on this moment in time. Not the past or future — just the simple present.

In the following sections, you use focused breathing methods to turn your attention inward, to your thoughts, feelings, and sensations, and find just the right moment to begin writing. I call this moment _the sweet spot_ for writing from mindfulness.

Focusing on breath

One of the most effective ways to quickly center yourself in the moment is to focus on your breathing. You can use a number of different breathing techniques to become centered and ready to begin your mindful journaling.

Do This

To find the breathing technique that works best to help you center in the present, follow these steps:

1. **Find a place where you can be undisturbed and sit or lie in a comfortable position.**

2. **Try the methods in the following sections to see which one works best for you.**

   Not all methods work equally well for everyone, so it's important to find one that you feel comfortable with and helps you relax and feel fully present.

TIP

After you find a method that you like, use this method each time to prepare for your mindful journaling session. It takes time and patience to perfect your practice, which you can most effectively accomplish by repeating the same method until it becomes part of your journaling ritual.

Focusing on your natural breathing rhythm

In this practice, you don't try to control your breathing. Simply notice your breath while it enters and leaves your body.

Do This

Follow these steps:

1. **Close your eyes and pay attention to the natural rise and fall of your chest and abdomen while you breathe.**

2. **Focus on the feeling of the air flowing in and flowing out.**

   If your mind wanders, bring it gently back to focus on your breathing.

3. **Stay focused on your breath until you feel centered and calm and fully present in the moment.**

   This may take from two to five minutes.

4. **Allow your attention to return to your surroundings; you are now prepared to begin mindful journaling.**

Using controlled breaths

If you have difficulty keeping your attention on your natural breathing patterns (as described in the previous exercise), engaging your mind by inhaling and exhaling for a specific number of counts, or beats, can help you maintain focus.

Do This

Follow these steps to focus on your breathing, which will in turn help you become centered and present:

1. **Gently close your eyes and take a deep inhale through your nostrils while you slowly count to four.**

   In for 1-2-3-4.

2. **Hold at the top of your breath for the count of two.**

   Hold for 1-2.

3. **Exhale through your mouth for four counts.**

   Out for 1-2-3-4.

4. **Hold again at the bottom for two counts.**

   Hold for 1-2.

5. **Continue repeating Steps 1 through 4.**

   Breathe in for four, hold for two, out for four, hold for two.

6. **While you count, focus on your breath as it moves through your body.**

   Observe the feeling of the air while it enters your nostrils and fills your lungs, what it feels like when you hold it at the top, and then again while it leaves your lungs and goes out your mouth, and how it feels while you hold it at the bottom.

   If your mind begins to wander, bring it gently back to your breath and begin to count again.

7. **Continue breathing in this way until you feel centered and calm and fully present in the moment.**

   This may take from two to five minutes.

8. **Allow your attention to return to your surroundings; you are now prepared to begin mindful journaling.**

Measuring with the heart

Like the technique described in the section "Focusing on your natural breathing rhythm," earlier in this chapter, this method has you breathe naturally — not short, long, or exaggerated.

Do This

Follow these steps to focus on your heartbeat as you breathe:

1. While you breathe naturally, count how many heart-beats you feel while you inhale.

2. Count the number of heartbeats while you exhale.

3. Continue counting heartbeats for each inhale and each exhale, noticing the rhythm of your heart and how it connects with your breath.

   You may notice your heart slowing as your breath naturally deepens. Or you may find that you inhale and exhale for different amounts of time (as counted by the beats of your heart). Or you may notice something else — there's no right or wrong.

4. Continue breathing and counting heartbeats until you feel centered, calm, and fully present in the moment.

   This may take from two to five minutes.

5. Allow your attention to return to your surroundings; you are now prepared to begin mindful journaling.

Breathing with alternate nostrils

Another method for centering yourself involves breathing through one nostril at a time.

Do This

Just follow these steps:

1. For this exercise, I recommend sitting in a chair or on a cushion that supports your spine to sit straight and tall.

   Sitting tall helps you draw breath deeper into your lungs.

2. Take two to three deep, slow breaths through both nostrils, pulling the breath deep so that your belly rises before your chest does.

3. Close off one nostril with your thumb.

4. Inhale slowly and deeply as before.

   Inhaling through only one nostril forces you to slow down. Notice how the air feels as it enters your nose and fills your lungs.

5. **Remove your thumb from your nostril.**

6. **Use your first finger to close off the opposing nostril.**

7. **Slowly exhale.**

   Notice how slowly you need to release the air. Breath out completely. Notice the warmth of your breath as it exits your nostril.

8. **Repeat Steps 2 through 6, switching nostrils for each inhale and exhale.**

   Continue breathing this way for two to five minutes, until you feel centered, peaceful, and fully present in the moment.

9. **Allow your attention to return to your surroundings; you are now prepared to begin mindful journaling.**

Finding the sweet spot: You're ready to write!

Mindful journaling is done from a place of inner quiet, when you are centered in the present moment, aware of your surroundings and thoughts, and not distracted by thoughts of the past or future.

Depending on your experience with being mindful, you may be able to center yourself quickly by taking a few deep breaths or meditating for a few minutes. Or you can perform a body scan as described in the "Body scanning: Tuning into physical sensations" section or use one of the methods in the "Focusing on breath" section (both sections appear earlier in this chapter).

Whichever method you use, when you reach a place of quiet peace, stay still and focused on that intense sense of presence. Notice what's happening in your body and around you. Notice your thoughts. Let them drift through your mind and don't follow any of them. Simply be with yourself.

While you remain in that place of inner quiet and peace, certain images or thoughts may begin to rise within you. You may also begin feeling the urge to write.

This is the sweet spot — the place to begin your mindful journaling.

Putting Mindful Journaling in Play

After you have some practice and feel comfortable with a few methods for raising awareness of and attention to the present, as outlined in the section "Centering on the Moment," earlier in this chapter, it's time for a complete mindful journaling session.

TIP

Find a comfortable sitting position in a quiet location and read through the entire instructions in the sections "Exploring Mindfulness and How to Become More Aware" and "Centering on the Moment," earlier in this chapter. Then, you can focus on your mindful journaling practice, rather than having to stop to read directions and then try to start again.

Gather your journaling tools — a pen or pencil, perhaps some colored pencils or markers. If you want, have your journal or notebook ready in case you have more to write than can fit in the space provided in this book.

For your mindful journaling session, follow the steps outlined in this section.

Step 1: Set your intention for the journaling session

You may not always have a specific purpose in mind. However, if you want to tap into your inner wisdom to answer a question or make a decision about something in your life, you can consciously set your intention at the start of your practice.

Do This

What is your intention for this session? What question do you want to answer or what decision do you need to make? Or maybe you simply want inner guidance about a specific situation. Write down your question or topic. Then, release it from your mind.

_____

_____

_____

TIP

If you don't have a specific intention for your session, you can skip this step.

Step 2: Focus your awareness in the present

To center yourself and bring your awareness to the present, use any of the breathing methods described in the section "Focusing on breath" earlier in this chapter.

Do This

To center yourself and focus your awareness in the present, follow these steps:

1. **Focus on your breath by using the breathing method of your choice.**

REMEMBER

If your mind begins to wander away from your breath, bring it gently back. Continue focusing on your breath for two to five minutes, until you feel completely calm and centered in the now (the present).

2. **Bring awareness to the sensations in your body.**

If you're using controlled breathing method, allow your breathing to return to a normal, natural rhythm.

3. **Notice any feelings, thoughts, and images as they float through your consciousness.**

    Don't linger on any particular images or thoughts; just notice them and then let them go.

4. **Continue in this state until you feel a deep, abiding sense of quiet and contentment — or until you feel an urge to write.**

    You have found the sweet spot and are ready to begin writing.

Step 3: Journal spontaneously

Journaling mindfully is usually spontaneous. It's free-writing, but because you're focused on the moment and not on the past or future, your inner wisdom and intuition can bubble to the surface more easily. You're more likely to be writing from a place of inner peace and equanimity and less likely to be writing out of pain or anxiety. So the nature or quality of what you write will be different from what you would write if you were not in a state of mindfulness.

TIP

If you want ideas for topics to write about, you can use mindful journaling prompts instead of the spontaneous journaling method. See the sidebar, "Inspiring prompts for mindful journaling" for specific ideas.

Do This

Follow these steps to journal:

1. **Remind yourself of your intention or the questions or topic you posed to yourself at the start of the session (refer to the earlier section "Step 1: Set your intention for the journaling session").**

2. **Write down the first thought that occurs to you in the space provided.**

    In the same way that you allowed your thoughts to simply float away while focusing your awareness (as discussed in the preceding section), allow your first thought to flow spontaneously through your fingers and onto the page.

Or, if you prefer, choose a prompt from the sidebar, "Inspiring Prompts for Mindful Journaling" and complete the sentence by writing down your first thought related to the prompt. Then, allow your thoughts and writing to flow freely.

3. **Continue writing until your thoughts have subsided.**

_____

_____

_____

_____

_____

_____

_____

_____

Step 4: Reflect on the process

At the end of each mindful journaling session, reflect on your experience of the writing process. This review-and-reflect process should only take a few minutes to complete.

Do This

Review what you wrote during your journaling session. Did you gain any new insights or wisdom related to your intention for journaling? How do you feel after writing? Write any final thoughts here:

_____

_____

_____

_____

_____

_____

INSPIRING PROMPTS FOR MINDFUL JOURNALING

When you come to your journaling session without a specific intention or topic to write about, journaling prompts come to the rescue. After bringing yourself into a state of mindfulness, select one of the following sentence-starting prompts that inspires or appeals to you and begin writing.

As you journal, stay calm and present, and allow your thoughts and writing to flow from your center. (You can also think of your center as your intuition or inner self.)

- Right now, I'm feeling . . .
- When I focus on my surroundings, I'm aware of . . .
- I believe that I can . . .
- When I think about my life, I feel . . .
- Things I noticed today include . . .
- I want to let go of . . .
- Things I'm gaining understanding about in my life right now are . . .
- The best advice I can give myself is . . .
- The things and people that most inspire me are . . .
- If I had a magic wand, I would . . .
- The ways I am kind to myself include . . .
- The person I am becoming is . . .
- I take care of myself by . . .
- The present moment teaches me . . .
- I show self-compassion when . . .

IN THIS CHAPTER

» **Understanding the purposes and benefits of a Bullet Journal**

» **Deciding if a Bullet Journal is right for you**

» **Setting up and organizing your first journal**

» **Getting into a groove with the Bullet method**

» **Finding different ways to put your Bullet Journal to work**

Chapter **7**

Getting Organized with a Bullet Journal

B ullet Journaling (or BuJo) is a unique form of journaling. It isn't a traditional cathartic type, such as reflective journaling (discussed in Chapter 5), where you explore your feelings and belief systems through writing. Rather, Bullet Journaling gives you a method for quickly logging events, tasks, goals, appointments, accomplishments, new ideas, and plans for the future. It's a way of keeping everything in one place, rather than having it stored in various random places, such as in e-mail, on sticky notes, in reminder apps, and so on. Think of Bullet Journaling as similar to keeping a diary, but with added structure.

THE BEGINNING OF BUJO

Ryder Carroll developed the Bullet Journal method as an organizational system in 2013 to help cope with his attention-deficit/hyperactivity disorder (ADHD), to organize his thinking and stay focused on what was important to him.

The system, also known as BuJo, worked so well, he began sharing it with friends and coworkers. To his surprise, it worked just as well for them, and he discovered it was remarkably flexible in how people could apply it for different needs and purposes. The method went viral after Carroll launched his website, Bullet Journal (https://bulletjournal.com), and was featured on the popular web log *Lifehacker* (https://lifehacker.com/) and the business magazine *Fast Company* (https://www.fastcompany.com/).

After going viral, the Bullet Journal method has helped thousands of people organize their lives and become more productive. In addition, Bullet Journalists have used the method to enhance creativity, practice mindfulness, document their lives, and develop healthy new habits.

In this chapter, you take a close look at the benefits of Bullet Journaling, figure out whether it's the right kind of journaling for you, and get step-by-step guidance on how to structure, start, and maintain a Bullet Journal.

TIP

You can use Bullet Journaling on its own or in addition to other journaling methods, such as reflective journaling (Chapter 5), mindful journaling (Chapter 6), creative journaling (Chapter 8), and gratitude journaling (Chapter 9).

Getting Acquainted with Bullet Journaling Benefits

According to creator Ryder Carroll, the Bullet Journaling method can help you get a grasp on where you are and what you want in life, prioritize the important stuff, and become more self-aware and intentional in the process of living.

BuJo benefits you by helping you to

>> Organize your thinking

>> Set and prioritize your goals and tasks

>> Focus on your top priorities

>> Reflect on your activities

I discuss each of these benefits in more detail in the following sections.

Organizing your thoughts

Part of the problem many people have with being organized is that they simply have too much to do and too much to keep track of every day. Trying to remember everything that you need to do and making good decisions requires understanding the significance of each task or project. And prioritizing your to-dos requires being able to organize all those tasks and ideas flying around in your mind.

Decluttering your mind

The first step to getting organized involves decluttering your mind by writing down all those ideas and tasks that you need to address. After you write them down, your mind can relax because it no longer has to try to remember it all. Capturing your thoughts in writing clears the mental clutter and allows you to organize and focus on what's truly important.

REMEMBER

This concept of decluttering and organizing is at the heart of the Bullet Journal method. For this reason, you do Bullet Journaling throughout the day, rather than once per day like other types of journaling. Here's how Bullet Journaling works throughout a typical day:

>> **In the morning:** Consider your day ahead and review or make your to-do list, note any events and appointments that you have on your schedule, and so on.

>> **During the day:** Record additional tasks, ideas, events, and notes and reactions about those events.

>> **In the evening:** Mark tasks completed, reflect on your day's events, and prepare for the next day.

The key to all of this journaling involves consistently decluttering your mind by writing down thoughts in your Bullet Journal when they come to you.

Processing your mental inventory

A great way to grasp how decluttering works is to start with Carroll's *mental inventory* process. In this activity, you write a list for each of the following three categories: What I'm currently working on, what I should be working on, and what I want to work on.

Here's an example:

>> What I'm currently working on:

- Retirement plan

- Cleaning out the garage

- Menu planning for the week

- Repainting the kids' bedroom

>> What I should be working on:

- Spring gardening plan

- Practicing the piano

- Regular exercise

>> What I want to work on:

- Learning Spanish

- Summer vacation plans

Do This

With the preceding example mental inventory in mind, think about your own life and write your lists in the space provided.

What I'm currently working on:

_____

_____

_____

_____

_____

What I should be working on:

_____

_____

_____

_____

_____

What I want to be working on:

_____

_____

_____

_____

_____

In completing this activity, you have experienced what it means to declutter your mind. This process of writing down all the things you are, should be, or want to be working on gets everything out of a need-to-remember status and on paper, which in turn allows you to prioritize and focus on what you truly want.

Setting and prioritizing goals

When you declutter your mind by writing down your project tasks and miscellaneous to-dos, you can then review and prioritize those tasks. You can also use that list to set time-based goals and get more accomplished by sharpening your focus on what's most important to you.

This section guides you through an activity to help prioritize a list of tasks.

You can use your list from the "Processing your mental inventory" activity in the previous section, or you can perform these steps for tasks on any to-do list.

Do This

Follow these steps to prioritize your mental inventory:

1. **For each of the items on your to-do list, ask the following two yes-or-no questions:**

   Is this item important to me or someone I love?

   Is this item necessary for living (housing, food, transportation, and so on)?

2. **Put an asterisk next to any item for which you answered yes to both questions.**

   Yes, it's important; and yes, it's necessary.

3. **Cross off any item for which you answered no to both questions.**

4. **Leave the items for which you answered yes to either question.**

   Yes, it's important, *or* yes, it's necessary, but not both.

In completing this activity, you have created a working list of goals that are already identified as high (items that have asterisks) or normal priority (items that were left as-is). You have also removed unnecessary activities (items that were crossed off).

If you decide to try Bullet Journaling (see "Determining whether Bullet Journaling works for you" later in this chapter), I'll show you how to transfer this list to your Bullet Journal and then how to manage your tasks in the section "Starting a Bullet Journal," also later in this chapter. Remember, you can always add or remove items from your list.

Focusing on what's important

People who have a strong ability to focus can fix their full attention on a task or complex set of tasks, while being able to shut out distractions such as music and people talking in the background. They're not procrastinators. They tend to be goal-oriented and highly productive, understand their priorities, and tackle one thing at a time, instead of trying to multitask.

If that paragraph doesn't sound like you — if you struggle with procrastination, completing tasks, or achieving your goals — you probably spend a great deal of time trying to get and maintain focus.

Bullet Journaling is a flexible system that can help you thoughtfully define and zero in on what you need to do each day, week, month, and year. A system that you can come back to any time you need to get back on track.

A consistent Bullet Journaling practice (discussed in "Starting a Bullet Journal" and "Practicing the Bullet Method Over Time" sections later in this chapter) helps you focus on what you want to accomplish by keeping your most important goals, tasks, and events in the forefront of your mind.

Reflecting on your activities

One of the most powerful benefits of Bullet Journaling is how it supports regular reflection on how you are living your life — on the activities you plan for and actually engage in.

Regular reflection sessions (daily, weekly, monthly) are baked into a Bullet Journaling practice. During these sessions you have the opportunity to look back on past events and actions, compare them with your plans and priorities, and then make adjustments as needed to steer your life in your desired direction, wherever that may be.

Reflection sessions and how to conduct them are described in more detail in the "Practicing the Bullet Method Over Time" section later in this chapter.

Exploring Your Reasons for Bullet Journaling

Before starting any new journaling method, it's important to clarify your motivations for wanting to try it. Bullet Journaling is no different.

To understand what draws you to Bullet Journaling, evaluate the organizational methods you're currently using and define what you hope to achieve when you become better organized.

Evaluating your current systems

How do you currently organize your flow of information and tasks? Consider the following kinds of professional and personal information that you need to coordinate and keep track of:

>> Books to read/movies to watch

>> Informational articles

>> E-mail

>> Social media

>> Projects

>> Tasks

>> Schedules

>> Goals

>> Ideas

>> Future plans

Do This

Think about what methods you use to track and organize all this information. List your methods here:

_____

_____

_____

_____

_____

Which of these methods or systems work the best to help you keep information organized and get things done? Now consider whether some of these methods could be improved by collecting the information in one place.

Deciding what you want to achieve

Although you can certainly see an increase in productivity as one outcome of Bullet Journaling, don't limit yourself to achieving specific goals. I'm asking a larger question: Who do you want to become, and what do you imagine your life could be like if you became more organized?

Do This

Take a moment to jot down your thoughts and ideas to help clarify your purpose for Bullet Journaling and consider what you want and who you want to be.

_____

_____

_____

_____

_____

_____

_____

_____

Determining whether Bullet Journaling works for you

You don't have to be diagnosed with attention-deficit/ hyperactivity disorder (ADHD) to be disorganized or have problems focusing on important priorities. Almost everyone these days is coping with constant distraction and difficulty getting things done. You might chalk it up to information overload — a consequence of living in our hyper-connected digital world. Or maybe it's a result of stress or lack of sleep.

So, how do you know whether the Bullet Journal method can work for you? First, answer these questions:

>> Do you tend to skim long passages of text, impatient to get to the end?

>> Does your mind flit from one idea or topic to the next?

>> Are you easily distracted by new information and ideas?

>> Do you tend to lose things, such as your keys or wallet?

>> Are you often late for meetings or appointments?

>> Do you have difficulty taking action toward and achieving your goals?

>> Do you often feel overwhelmed by life and responsibilities?

>> Do you have trouble remembering important events or information?

>> Do you ever call yourself a procrastinator?

If you answered yes to three or more of the preceding questions, Bullet Journaling might be the right method for you. Bullet Journaling utilizes consistent mind decluttering — ensuring that all those stray thoughts, distractions, and things you want to remember are recorded — and then helps you organize all that information in a way that is useful and actionable.

Starting a Bullet Journal

Starting your Bullet Journal is a straightforward process. First, it's important to understand how the method works, what you need to get started, and some of the terms that are commonly used.

Assembling supplies

When you're ready to start a Bullet Journal, in addition to this book you need a journal or notebook and a comfortable pen or pencil.

TIP

Most Bullet Journalists prefer either blank pages or pages that have a grid pattern, as shown in Figure 7-1. But any journal, lined or unlined, also works. For the most flexibility, you can start Bullet Journaling using an inexpensive blank notebook. As you use your journal, you'll discover how you like to work with it, and you can then experiment with other page designs.

FIGURE 7-1:
Pages of a Bullet Journal that have a dot-grid.

Whatever type of page you prefer, make the notebook you choose for your Bullet Journal small enough to carry with you throughout your day, but large enough to write comfortably in. Typical Bullet Journals sold online are approximately 5.25-x-8 inches.

Bullet Journaling by hand has many benefits, but even if you prefer to use digital tools, start with a paper journal. It's important to work with Bullet Journaling on paper to grasp all of its methods and concepts. Then, when you're familiar with Bullet Journaling as it was originally designed, you can more easily adapt a digital note-taking application or purchase a BuJo-specific application.

Indexing entries

The first, and perhaps most essential, part of a Bullet Journal is its index. You maintain the index (essentially, a table of contents) in the first pages of the journal. When you add entries to your journal, number the pages (some journals come with pages already numbered) and fill out your journal's index with a topic title and page number for each topic.

REMEMBER

Life doesn't happen in a neat, linear order. Nor do our ideas. While you're recording an event that occurred today, you might get an idea for an ongoing project. The beauty of indexing your entries is that you don't have to search through your journal to find previous entries or ideas. Your index enables you to always find what you want, when you want it.

Do This

Dedicate the first four pages of your journal to your index. Open your journal and number the first four pages in the way that appeals to you — top corners, bottom corners, or bottom center, for example. Then title each page with the word "Index" at the top.

Creating your first collections: Daily, monthly, and future logs

Bullet Journaling is a modular system. You collect and organize information by topic, and each topic is considered a *collection*.

Examples of collections you can use in your Journal include your daily, monthly, and future logs (more about these logs in the following sections). You can also create collections for goals, projects, habit tracking, information gathering, books read, courses taken — well, pretty much anything you can think of.

When you create each collection, you list the title and page number(s) in your index.

Figure 7-2 shows an example of an index that contains some entries.

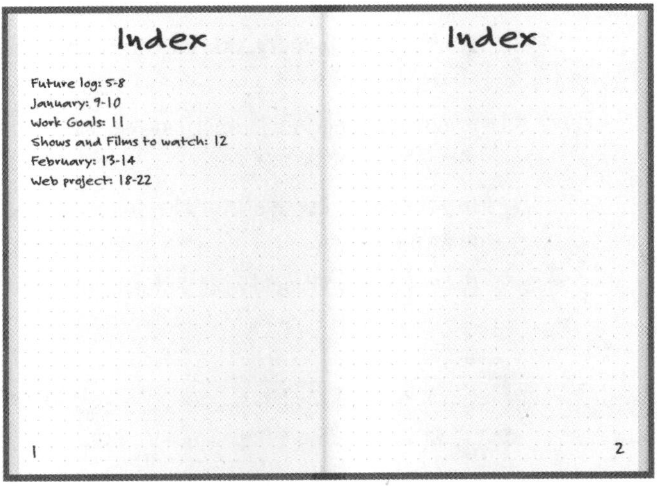

Index

Future log: 5-8
January: 9-10
Work Goals: 11
Shows and Films to watch: 12
February: 13-14
Web project: 18-22

Index

1   2

FIGURE 7-2:
Index pages
that contain
entries.

Setting up a future log

After your index, reserve the next set of pages for your future log. You can design a future log in different ways — devoting one month, two months, three months, or more per page. It depends on how busy your life is and how much space you think you'll need. A common design is three months per page, using four pages for 12 months; check out the following Do This exercise for more info.

You use your future log for events and tasks that occur outside of the current month. For example, if you have a due date or a special event six months from now, simply jot it down in the appropriate month in your future log.

I provide more details about how to use your future log in the section "Practicing the Bullet Method Over Time," later in this chapter.

Do This

To set up your future log with three months per page, follow these steps:

1. **Open your journal and number pages 5 through 8.**

2. **Title each page with the words "Future Log" at the top.**

3. **Divide each page into thirds horizontally.**

4. **Starting with January, title each section by month, as shown in Figure 7-3.**

   If you're starting your journal mid-year, start with the month that follows the current one.

5. **In your index, list the future log followed by a colon and the page numbers.**

   For example, you could write "Future Log: 5–8."

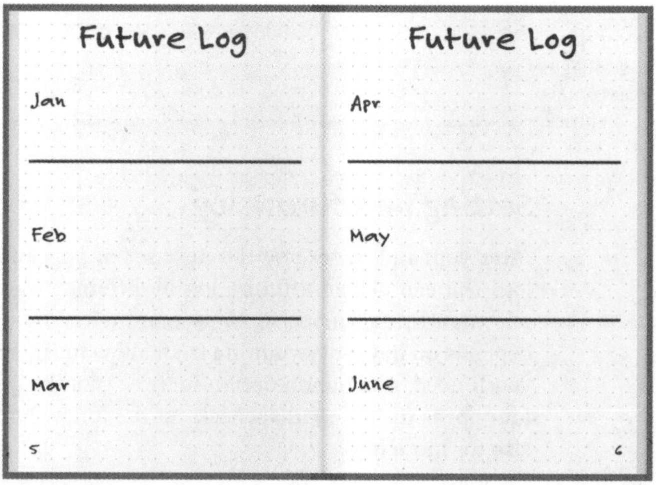

FIGURE 7-3: The first two pages of a future log.

Future Log

Jan

Feb

Mar

5

Future Log

Apr

May

June

6

Setting up a monthly log

After you create your future log (see the preceding section), create a monthly log for the current month. Monthly logs take one full spread. The left page is your calendar page, and the right page is used to list tasks, as shown in Figure 7-4.

January	January
1 M	• Take Christmas stuff to storage
2 T	• Update financial plan
3 W	• Set goals for year
4 Th	• Submit vacation days off
5 F	• Make dentist appt

FIGURE 7-4: Example of a monthly log spread.

Do This

To create your monthly log, follow these steps:

1. Open your journal and number pages 9 and 10.

2. Title each page with the name of the current month at the top.

3. On the left page, number all the days of the month vertically down the left side of the page, followed by the first letter of the day of the week.

   Leave a bit of a margin on the left so that you have room to add symbols to indicate important events. (You can get some ideas for what symbols to use and how to use them in the section "Using symbols to identify entry types," later in this chapter.)

4. Add your monthly log title (the name of the month) and page numbers to the index, as shown in Figure 7-2.

Setting up a daily log

Your daily log is the engine of your journal. It's where you track all your tasks and write down everything that comes into your head throughout the day that you want to remember for later. This process is known as *rapid logging*.

The point of rapid logging is to constantly declutter your mind by writing things down when they occur to you.

Do This

To create a daily log, simply find the next available page in your journal, write the day's date and day of the week at the top, and number the page.

You don't add daily logs to the index, and each log doesn't need to be on a separate page. If a daily log takes up only one-half page, you can start the next day's log on the same page. In the same way, if a daily log takes up two pages, start the next day's log on the next available page.

Figure 7-5 shows an example of a completed daily log. Each item has a symbol in front of it. Find out how to use these symbols in the following section.

Using symbols to identify entry types

Symbols let you quickly identify the entry type in your Bullet Journal. The most typical entry types are *tasks* (things that need to be done), notes, and *events* (something that will or has occurred).

While you read the following descriptions, refer back to Figure 7-5 to see how the symbols are used in the example daily log:

>> **Bullet (•):** Tasks

>> **Asterisk (*):** High-priority tasks

>> **X:** A completed task

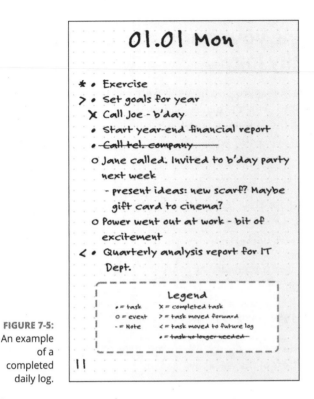

FIGURE 7-5: An example of a completed daily log.

>> **Right arrow (>):** A task that has been moved forward into your next monthly log or into a specific collection

>> **Left arrow (<):** A task that has been moved backward in your journal, into your future log

>> **Cross out (task):** A task that you decide is no longer important

>> **Dash (–):** Notes

You can include notes with tasks or events, or enter on their own when you need to jot down an idea.

>> **Circle (O):** Events

Events are anything that happened (or that you're planning to happen) that you want to record.

You can also create and use other symbols, as needed. For example, you can use a triangle (Δ) or an exclamation point (!) for notes that indicate "aha" moments or ideas.

Trying your hand at creating a daily log

To help you appreciate how the daily log and its symbols work, it's best to get some hands-on practice. This section guides you through the process of creating a daily log and using symbols to identify each entry type.

Do This

In the space provided, practice creating a daily log. You can use real tasks and events for today, or you can make them up for the purpose of this exercise.

If you need a reminder as to what a completed daily log might look like, refer to Figure 7-5.

Follow these steps to create your first daily log:

1. **Title your daily log with today's date and the first two letters of the weekday.**

   For example, you might write: "03.31 TH."

2. **Below the date, list five tasks and mark each one with a preceding bullet (•).**

3. **List two events, preceded by circles (O).**

   An event could be an appointment, meeting, party, phone call, or anything that happened during the day that you want to remember.

4. **Make a note about the event, preceded by a dash (–).**

   Your note could be about something in the future that you want to remember to say or bring. It could also be a look back at something someone said, how an event went, or inspirational ideas that came up during a conversation.

5. **Write down a few other notes or thoughts that could apply to your hypothetical day, indicating each with a dash (–).**

If this were your actual daily log, you'd add to it throughout your day, as needed. But the preceding steps have you create enough entries for the purpose of this and the following exercise.

Pretend you've come to the end of your day and you want to organize and reflect for the following day. Follow these steps with your daily log:

1. **Mark two tasks as completed by putting an X over each bullet.**

2. **Select one task to migrate to tomorrow's daily log and mark it with a right arrow (>).**

   If this were your actual journal, you'd also create the next day's daily log and rewrite the task there.

3. **Select one task to move to a future month in your future log and mark the task with a left arrow (<).**

   Again, if this were your actual journal, you'd also rewrite the task in the appropriate month of your future log.

4. **Mark one task as no longer needed by crossing it out (drawing a line through it).**

5. **Add a note to one of the day's events, preceded by a dash (-).**

   How did the event go? Here, you would note impressions of the event or any related ideas you want to remember.

Practicing the Bullet Method Over Time

Keep some general principles in mind when you begin practicing the Bullet Journaling method. Although the section "Starting a Bullet Journal," earlier in this chapter, focuses on the mechanics of Bullet Journaling, remember that this method is about more than to-do lists and schedules.

Your Bullet Journal is a place to collect all the stray bits of information in your life and to organize them. It's a tool for reflection, for thinking about what's most important to you, and for providing insight into your daily experiences and patterns.

If you approach it with curiosity, your Bullet Journal can be a valuable part of your personal development. It's the vehicle for clarifying both the What and the Why of everything you do and for raising awareness about what's meaningful to you so that you can live your life by your highest beliefs and principles.

Creating a routine

Bullet Journaling is done throughout the day, with reflection periods occurring at the start and/or end of each day, week, and month.

The following sections show you what a typical routine might look like. Adapt these routines to suit your needs.

Daily routine

The daily routine described here can help you get started with Bullet Journaling. Once you've become comfortable with the journaling activities and established core habits, you can adapt the routine to work best with your preferences and schedule.

In the morning, preferably before you've truly started your day (upon waking, before or after breakfast, or before starting work):

>> Add planned tasks and events.

>> Mark the high priority tasks with asterisks.

>> Enter notes and reminders to yourself.

Throughout the day, carry your journal with you and refer to it periodically:

>> Add tasks and notes when they occur to you (this is called *rapid logging*) in your daily log.

>> Add events that occur during the day and any related notes.

>> Record any ideas and thoughts you want to remember.

You can mark tasks complete by putting Xs over their bullets when you finish them, or you can wait until the end of the day, during your evening reflection period. (I talk about the symbols to use in your Bullet Journal in the section "Using symbols to identify entry types," earlier in this chapter.)

Your daily log helps you keep your mind uncluttered because you write everything down that you want to remember. You organize these items during your evening reflection period.

During your evening reflection, which can be done at the end of your workday or while you're winding down before bed:

>> Review your daily log, mark tasks complete, and enter any final events and notes.

>> Migrate tasks and events relevant to future dates in the current month to your monthly log.

>> Move tasks and events relevant to future months to your future log.

You can complete the following actions either in the evening or during your morning reflection the following day:

>> Create tomorrow's daily log. Check out the section "Creating your first collections: Daily, monthly, and future logs" earlier in this chapter for guidance.

>> Copy (migrate) relevant events and tasks from your monthly log and any incomplete tasks from the day you're closing to the following day's log.

REMEMBER

While you review your journal, take the time to think about each item. Ask yourself whether the task or event is still important to you and why you're doing it. If a task has become unimportant, then don't migrate it; simply cross it out. If a scheduled event no longer seems worth your time, cancel it, if possible.

Weekly routine

Establish a weekly reflection session to review and evaluate the week prior and stay on track with all your goals, tasks, and events. I like to conduct my weekly reflection on Sunday evenings, while things are winding down for the current week and my mind is turning toward plans for the upcoming week.

Other popular days for weekly reflection times include Friday afternoons and Monday mornings. Choose what works best for you and schedule it on your calendar.

During your weekly reflection

>> **Review your accomplishments.** Acknowledge and allow yourself to feel good about what you've accomplished during the week.

>> **Review your daily logs.** Are there incomplete tasks that tend to be continually migrated forward to the next day? If so, look more deeply into those tasks:

  ● *Consider each task.* Is the task still important to you, something you really want to do? If not, maybe it's no longer relevant and can simply be crossed off.

  ● *Consider your motivations.* If the task is still important in some way, ask yourself why you're procrastinating. Either make it a higher priority or see if you can delegate or hire someone else to do it.

>> **Review your notes.** Do your notes include ideas that can be incorporated into existing goals or projects, or added as a new collection? (Continue to the section "Adding new collections," later in this chapter, to find out about creating collections.)

GETTING CREATIVE WITH BULLETS

Just as the uses for Bullet Journaling are endless, so are the ways you can make it uniquely your own.

Although the original Bullet Journal method uses simple bullets and symbols to indicate the types and status of different entries, Bullet Journalists all over the world have made BuJo their own by creating custom symbols to suit their needs.

For example, one woman created an easily drawn symbol for every area of her life: a tiny dumbbell for exercise, an ornate dollar sign for financial notes, a small house for household and home-related tasks, a flower for gardening, and a heart for relationships. Using these symbols, she can quickly scan a day or a week to see which areas of her life she has been more focused on. Consider creating custom icons for your own life.

Using colors is another way to enhance the Bullet Journaling experience. You can use colors to indicate mood or expand the visual impact of a habit tracker.

Monthly routine

Toward the end of each month, set aside some time to do a monthly reflection:

>> Create a new monthly log for the upcoming month.

>> Migrate events and tasks from your future log to the monthly log.

>> Review your previous month's logs. Reflect on what you observe.

- Are certain tasks getting constantly pushed to the bottom of the list? As described earlier in the "Weekly routine" section, decide if the task is still important to you or if it should be crossed off. If still important, examine your motivation for keeping it on the list.

- Review your notes and decide if you want to migrate any of them to your future, monthly, or daily logs. Or perhaps you have ideas for projects or events that merit their own collections (See the "Adding new collections" section, which follows this one.)

- What knowledge did you gain from last month's experiences that you can apply going forward? Jot ideas down in your current day's log. Or create a special collection for "Knowledge Gained" (see the following section for how to add a new collection) where you can gather your discoveries.

Adding new collections

In addition to future, monthly, and daily logs — which are types of collections — you can add collections to your journal for any topic you can dream up. For example, you can have collections for projects, goals, class notes, creative ideas, and so on. Reasons for collections are unlimited and depend simply on what's happening in your life and how you want to organize it.

One common reason for a collection (or collections) is to track goals. You can have one collection for all your goals, or you can have separate collections for work and personal goals, for example.

If a goal has multiple steps or is a complex project, you can create a collection dedicated to that goal. For example, I have a goal to expand my vegetable garden this spring. I created a Vegetable Garden collection in my journal and broke down what I needed to do into a list of manageable tasks. I migrate garden tasks to my daily, monthly, and future logs, as appropriate. I also include a sketch of my garden plans and add notes during the spring and summer to record the garden's progress: what I'm planting, when I've fertilized, and so on.

Do This

To create a Goals collection, follow these steps:

1. **Go to the next blank page in your journal and add the title Goals to the top of the page.**

2. **Copy your list of goals from the mental inventory exercise, and include the asterisks next to the items you deemed high priority.**

   I explain this exercise in the section "Processing your mental inventory," earlier in this chapter.

3. **Add the Goals collection to your index.**

   For example, you can name it simply Goals: [page#].

If you'd rather create a collection for each type of goal you've set, or for each goal that requires multiple tasks to complete, then title and index each collection separately. Here's how:

1. **Go to the next blank page in your journal and title it with the name of your goal or collection.**

   For example, you might decide to create a collection that includes several work-related goals. In this case you could title the page Work Goals.

2. **Brainstorm a list of tasks that you need to accomplish to achieve your goal.**

   You can always revise this list later.

3. **Add the collection name and page number(s) to the index.**

4. **Repeat Steps 1 and 3 for each type of goal that requires multiple tasks.**

Indexing additional pages

Remember to add the title of each new monthly log and collection to your index, along with the page numbers.

Because you don't know how many pages a collection may take, you can continue a collection on a discontinuous page. To easily know on which page a collection is continued, add the page number to the previous page.

For example, if you started a project collection on pages 24 and 25 of your Bullet Journal, and that collection spills over to the next available page in your journal, which happens to be page 42, you notate page 42 just before your page number on page 25, like this: 42/25. Doing so lets you know to flip ahead to page 42 for the rest of that collection. Figure 7-6 shows an example of how to notate a continuation in your index.

Writing the continuation page before the existing page number is typical BuJo practice, as taught originally by Bullet Journal creator Ryder Carroll. But your journal belongs to you and you can feel free to modify it in any way you like. If typical practice doesn't work for you, perhaps because of where you've placed your page numbering, you can reverse the order (from 42/25 to 25/42). Just be consistent throughout your journal to avoid confusion later.

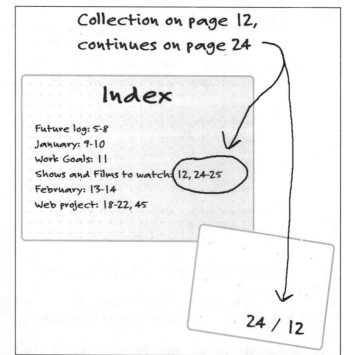

FIGURE 7-6:
Indicate the page number in your index when continuing a collection later in your journal.

Exploring Other Ways to Use Bullet Journaling

Future, monthly, and daily logs and goals are just the beginning of ways that you can use Bullet Journaling. As discussed earlier in this chapter, you can use your Bullet Journal to track projects, ideas, quotes, and more. The following sections outline additional collection ideas you might want to use your journal for.

Tracking your habits

Many people use Bullet Journaling to track habits that they want to encourage or be more aware of in their lives.

You can track any behavior you want to start. For example, you might want to start walking five days a week or practice piano daily. A habit tracker makes you more accountable by acting as a reminder and providing a place to document your success at integrating your desired actions or behaviors in your life. It helps you become more mindful about your daily habits.

Or perhaps you want to break a habit, but in order to do so you need to have a better understanding and awareness of how often you do it, and under what circumstances. A habit tracker can help.

A *habit tracker* is a page or spread (*collection*) in your journal in which you track single or multiple habits. Some of the things Bullet Journalists have tracked include

>> Eating

>> Exercise

>> Sleep

>> Practicing new skills (musical, artistic, and so on)

>> Writing or journaling

>> Reading

>> Self-care habits

You can track just about any regular action or behavior. If you search online for *Bullet Journal habit tracker*, you can find many examples of how others have created trackers that work for them. You can adopt an existing idea or create one of your own. Figure 7-7 shows you an example of a habit tracker that tracks multiple habits using a simple table.

Habits	M	T	W	Th	F	Sa	Su
Exercise	✓	✓	✓	✓	-	✓	✓
Practice Piano	✓	-	✓	-	✓	-	✓
Journal	—	✓	✓	✓	—	✓	—
Meditate	✓	✓	✓	✓	—	✓	—

FIGURE 7-7: An example of a simple habit tracker.

Improving mental health

You can use Bullet Journaling to document your moods, track specific emotions (such as anxiety or depression), and maintain lists of health-affirming events (such as compliments, good days, and positive interactions).

You can use your journal to focus on the positive in life with a Gratitude collection, where you keep a running list of all the things and people in your life for which you're grateful. Or create a Mindfulness collection, where you list ways to increase your sense of presence and live more mindfully.

Planning the future

By organizing your tasks and information into collections, your Bullet Journal can simplify planning for any event or project. Here are a few creative ideas for planning in your journal:

>> A wedding or party

>> Meals

>> Budget

>> Travel

>> Training and exercise

Truly, the list of uses for your Bullet Journal is nearly infinite, limited only by your needs and imagination.

IN THIS CHAPTER

» **Understanding the purpose and benefits of creative journaling**

» **Finding freedom in play**

» **Knowing what you need to begin**

» **Trying out different methods of creative journaling**

» **Practicing with creative journaling prompts**

Chapter **8**

Expressing Yourself through Creative Journaling

long with helping you process events, thoughts, emotions, and belief systems, journaling can be a powerful tool for creative development and expression. In addition to the writing-based techniques introduced in Chapters 5, 6, and 7, creative journaling can help you generate and collect ideas, solve problems, and express thoughts and feelings that are difficult to put to words.

Creative journaling blends artistic and traditional journaling techniques to help you delve into and communicate your deepest thoughts and emotions. Adding drawing, doodling, painting, and other visual forms of expression frees you from verbal constraints and expands your methods for self-expression and exploration.

Whatever your passion — from writing to crafting to engineering — creative journaling can help you nurture and enhance your creativity while exploring and developing ideas in a safe space, free of external and internal criticism.

In this chapter, I introduce you to a variety of techniques that you can use in your creative journal.

Unlocking Your Creativity

Creative journaling gives you a place to explore and strengthen your inner creative force. Use it to develop your imagination, sketching out new and novel ideas, or to enhance problem-solving skills. Play with visual art forms, including writing, drawing and painting, and photography.

You have almost no limit to what you can explore in your creative journal. Here are a few things you can do with it:

>> Brainstorm ideas

>> Solve problems

>> Practice your writing craft

>> Play with poetry

>> Color your inner world

>> Create a scrapbook

>> Test ideas and concepts

Think about ways that you want to express your own creativity. What can you add to this list?

Freeing your mind from preconceived notions

The first thing you need to do when creative journaling is free yourself from two ideas. Remember that

» Journaling isn't always writing.

» Journals can do more than help you process thoughts and emotions or keep track of events in your life.

There are no hard and fast rules to journaling, and that goes double for creative journaling. What you want to use your journal for and how you want to structure it — if you want any structure at all — is entirely up to you.

Revealing your assumptions about journaling

Because assumptions are beliefs that form the foundation of other thoughts, people are usually unaware of them. Don't think you have any assumptions about journaling? Bring your assumptions to the surface with the following activity.

Do This

Quickly, and without thinking about it, write down everything you know about the right way to journal:

_____

_____

_____

_____

_____

_____

Did you find that you do indeed have some inner rules about journaling?

Now review your list and, for each item, say out loud, "This is *one* way to journal, not the *right* way to journal."

REMEMBER

The only way you can be free to come up with new ways of doing things (in life and in journaling) is to let go of the notion that there is a right or wrong way to go about it. There is only the way you *choose* to do it.

Acknowledging your creativity

Do you think you're not a very creative person when compared with other people you know?

I ask because many people carry around the idea that some humans are born with the ability to be creative and that others . . . well, they just don't have it. I'd like to disabuse you of that idea.

Creativity is inherent in every single human on the planet, and that includes you. Creativity is also a bit like a muscle — you have to exercise it to develop it and make it strong. People you consider creative geniuses have simply had the time, confidence, and support to develop their natural creativity.

Do This

To test how you truly feel about your creativity, look in the mirror and say aloud to yourself, "I am a creative person. I can develop my creative abilities to express myself in new and novel ways."

How do you react while you're making this statement to yourself? Do you truly believe what you're saying? Does it feel exactly right, or does some part of you think that you're pretending?

If you feel at ease making a positive statement about your creativity, you may look forward to trying new ways to express yourself. On the other hand, if you feel that saying you're creative is an overstatement, that you're not really all that creative, don't worry — you just need a little practice to feel more comfortable with the idea.

Releasing inhibitions to self-expression

A common barrier to expressing yourself creatively is inhibition — that self-conscious feeling that holds you back from being able to relax and be yourself. It prevents you from doing something that comes naturally to you but for which you're afraid others might judge you negatively. These feelings can hold you back, even when expressing yourself privately in your journal.

Of course, some inhibitions are healthy. They help you control your emotions and prevent acting out in ways that you might regret later, such as calling someone names because you're angry. But if you find yourself holding back from trying new things because you feel insecure, inadequate, or "not creative enough," it's time to let go of those inhibitions.

That can be easier said than done because inhibitions arise from feelings that aren't always rational.

Check out the following sections that help you to release any inhibitions that might be holding you back from developing your creative muscle.

Acknowledge your inhibitions

The first step to releasing your inhibitions is to identify and acknowledge them. After all, how can you release something you're not aware of?

Do This

Think about how you feel about yourself, creatively speaking. Have you always wanted to draw or paint but thought you had no talent? Or perhaps you want to play an instrument, act, or start a new craft, but you're too embarrassed about asking for help to get started.

List four creative activities or ways of expressing yourself that you've been nervous about trying:

_____

_____

_____

_____

Reflect on why you feel the way you do

Think about the factors in your life that led you to view your creative abilities the way you do.

Do This

Ask yourself what most worries you about attempting to become more creative, and write your answer in the space provided.

_____

_____

_____

_____

_____

_____

Use positive affirmations to challenge old ideas

An *affirmation* is a positive statement designed to counter negative thoughts. People tend to believe the things they keep repeating to themselves. In the same way, affirmations work through repetition.

Do This

Write down three to five positive affirmations that challenge the idea that you're not creative or artistic. For best success, build your affirmations on what you know and believe. For example, "I know I am creative because I'm a good problem solver." Or, "I have the ability to be creative."

_____

_____

_____

_____

_____

_____

_____

_____

Do something out of your comfort zone

Inhibitions keep us rooted in our comfort zones, where we know we can succeed. When you do something out of that comfort zone, you might feel insecure and inhibited in some way. Practice acknowledging your feelings and then doing what's uncomfortable anyway. Forcing yourself to push past your inhibitions increases your confidence in your ability to create in new ways.

Do This

When it comes to expressing yourself with art, what's outside your comfort zone? Write down two small actions you can take that would push you just slightly out of your comfort zone. For example, if you feel inhibited about drawing, you could try sketching an object that has a simple shape.

_____

_____

_____

_____

Inviting your muse

In Greek mythology, nine sister goddesses presided over song, poetry, art, and science, and they were responsible for human inspiration.

It's commonly thought that inspiration (a _muse_) is necessary for creativity. However, I would turn that idea on its head: For inspiration to show up, you must first apply yourself to your art.

When you sit down and begin the work of creating, you fire up your mind, which automatically lights up connections, ideas, and insights.

Think of it like a creativity party. You're the host, and your muse is an honored guest. You set the time and place; provide the decorations, the food and drinks, and the entertainment; and show up before your guests.

When you sit down with your creativity journal, you're hosting that party. So, have confidence in yourself, invite your muse along, and see what happens.

Making Your Own Rules

When I talk about the other forms of journaling in this book, I give you specific techniques and structures for each type of journaling. And each of those techniques helps you gain the most for that type of journaling.

For example, with reflective journaling (covered in Chapter 5), you write to prompts that help you think more deeply about what's going on in your heart and mind in response to life events. And Bullet Journaling is structured to organize your thinking and your life. (Flip to Chapter 7 for more about Bullet Journaling.) However, even the most structured forms of journaling allow for a great deal of personalization and flexibility.

FREEING YOUR PLAYFUL SIDE

Why do children play? Play is an essential part of mental, emotional, and physical development for humans and other baby mammals. When they play, children develop essential skills while having fun. Through early games such as peekaboo and playing house, children figure out how to interact socially and think critically. They get to practice roles and skills that they'll use later in life.

Think back on your own childhood. What were some of the games you played with other children and by yourself? As you grew older and began taking on the responsibilities of adulthood, did you sometimes forget how to play? If so, you're not alone. You're taught that mature adults aren't supposed to play — or that play (recreational sports, video games, card games, and so on) should be partitioned off from the more serious matters of life. Of course, adults who do like to play sports or pretend games, such as Dungeons & Dragons, can find like-minded adults to play with at structured times and locations, but spontaneously getting engrossed in and acting out an imaginary world like children do would be impractical (not to mention socially awkward) in most adult social settings.

For most adults, play is often relegated to specific, structured times and places and takes second place to the serious matters of life. Creative journaling, when approached with an open mind and curiosity, can help you regain and free up that oh-so-important spontaneous playful side. And with play comes all of its benefits.

Play is important not only for children; it's important for adults, too. You play because it's fun and brings you pleasure. It's voluntary — not tied to responsibility — and done for its own sake. The very act of playing is its own reward and more important than the outcome.

Here are a few of the benefits of reintroducing play into your life through creative journaling:

- Helps you practice new skills in a non-threatening environment
- Releases endorphins and reduces stress
- Expends excess energy
- Literally stimulates brain cell growth and improves memory
- Brings you into the present moment (increasing mindfulness)
- Connects you to your inner sense of joy
- Develops confidence
- Triggers creativity
- Expands the imagination

Creative journaling is completely open-ended and not structured at all. In this form of journaling, you decide what you want to do. You write your own rules — that is, if you want any rules at all.

Sometimes, though, starting a journaling method that's completely open-ended can feel a little overwhelming. You might be asking, "How do I do this? Where do I start?" Or, "How can I begin if I don't know what I'm supposed to do?"

No need to worry. In the following sections, I guide you through figuring out your initial purpose for creative journaling, which will help you decide how you want to express yourself and which tools you want to use (see "Collecting Creative Journaling Tools and Materials" later in this chapter).

Establishing your purpose

Because you're reading this chapter, you probably have a pretty good idea of what's drawing you to the idea of a creative journal. Maybe you like journaling, but words just aren't enough, and you want to add pictures, color, or other ways of expressing yourself. Or perhaps you want to develop creative skills that you can draw upon in your work or daily life.

Knowing what you want to get out of creative journaling can guide you while you begin working with your journal.

Do This

To help you articulate your purpose, complete the following sentence: "I want to start a creative journal because . . ."

_____

_____

_____

_____

Dig a little deeper. Why do you want what you wrote in the preceding statement? What do you envision you can gain from it? Write your answers in the space provided.

_____

_____

_____

_____

_____

_____

_____

Deciding what "visual expression" means to you

When you consider the idea of *visual expression*, what do you picture? Think about all the ways humans have expressed themselves visually throughout history:

» Cave paintings

» Paintings on canvas

» Drawings and sketches

» Sculptures

» Graphs and charts (visual representations of statistics)

» Photography

» Crafts that have a visual as well as practical aesthetic

Any time you represent ideas and feelings by using visual and/or physical media, you evoke and communicate things that words, by themselves, can't convey. Visual media can be flat or three-dimensional, and tactile, as well as visual.

TAPPING INTO YOUR INNER CHILD

Maybe you've forgotten — just a little — *how* to let go of seriousness and allow yourself to play.

The key is to tap back into your inner child — the you who used to have so much fun playing. If the concept of tapping into your inner child seems "woo-woo," or irrational, bear with me. I guarantee that if you encourage that part of you to surface and be expressed in your life, you can have more fun, feel more joyful, and experience enhanced self-awareness.

Here's a list of things you can do to resurrect your inner playful self to prepare for creative journaling:

- Look at old photos to bring back memories from your childhood.

- Do something silly, such as giving an object an imaginary voice and having it tell you about its day.

- Play a physical sport or game you used to play as a child.

- Spend some time playing with kids.

- Make playdough food. (Just don't eat it!)

- Finger paint.

- Lie on your back outside and find shapes in the clouds.

- Go to the beach or park, and make a sand castle. (Take buckets and shovels with you.)

- The next time it rains, put on your rain boots and splash in the puddles.

- Treat yourself to something you used to love as a child — cotton candy or a ginormous ice cream cone.

Do This

Think about the kinds of visual expression that most appeal to you. Then, write your answer to this question: In what ways do you imagine expressing yourself visually through journaling?

_____

_____

_____

_____

Write about the ways in which visually expressing your feelings and thoughts could enhance your creative processes:

_____

_____

_____

_____

Collecting Creative Journaling Tools and Materials

Which tools and materials you need for creative journaling depends on what type of creative journaling you want to do.

You can stick to writing, using your creative journal for brainstorming, problem solving, ideas, and creative writing practice — all in words. In this case, you need only a notebook and pen, or a computer or electronic device.

But, for the sake of the discussion in the following sections, I'm going to assume that you're looking to express yourself by using more than words. Maybe words, *and* images, *and* doodles. Maybe you want to add color, sketching with pencils or markers, or washing the page with watercolor.

Starting simply

I always recommend starting any journaling endeavor simply, using a few basic tools. For creative journaling, these tools include

>> **A blank, unlined journal or notebook.** You need thick paper that won't bleed color through to the other side (see the section "Selecting the right notebook," later in this chapter). Choose a notebook that can lie flat when open. I like spiral bound notebooks for this purpose.

>> **Colored drawing utensils.** Ultrafine markers, colored pencils, gel pens, and crayons are all good choices. They are generally inexpensive, easy to use, and come in a wide variety of colors.

>> **Your favorite writing utensil.** In case you want to add writing to the page.

Expanding your toolkit

After you get a little experience using your basic tools (discussed in the preceding section), you might want to begin adding more to your creative journaling fun. Here are a few ideas for additional supplies:

>> Decorative rubber stamps and ink

>> Materials for collages, including glue sticks, ribbons, scraps of paper or cloth, magazine clippings, and photos

>> Painting supplies, including watercolor or acrylic paints, and brushes. You may also want to have white gesso on hand to prep the page. *Gesso* is a primer coating that will prevent paint from bleeding through the page — which can sometimes occur even with thick papers.

>> Oil pastels

>> Glitter

>> Stickers

Deciding which mode to use

Like other forms of journaling, you can keep a paper or digital creative journal. However, I strongly recommend using paper while you're beginning to explore creative journaling. (Flip to Chapter 3 for a discussion of paper versus digital journaling methods.)

Paper provides an organic medium on which to begin your creativity journey. Working with paper and physical supplies encourages a sense of play, and the tactile sensations provide satisfying feedback to your mind and body. It can also sometimes be messy — something to consider when deciding which mode to start with — but then, creativity itself is pretty messy. Messiness is just part of the process.

For those who prefer or need to journal digitally, you'll be happy to know that everything you can do in a paper journal, you can do in a digital journal: doodle, color, paint, paste images, and so on. All of the supplies discussed in the section "Starting simply," earlier in this chapter, and the preceding section have digital equivalents.

Yet, journaling digitally has its downsides: A digital journal requires different tools and techniques, may use multiple applications, and can come with a steep learning curve. And, of course, digital apps lack the tactile feedback.

In addition, when you go the digital route, you face the danger of getting so caught up in figuring out how to use the applications that it restricts your ability to freely express yourself.

On the other hand, if you're already tech-savvy and prepared to tackle the learning curve, you might find that a creative digital journal is more flexible and adaptable for your unique brand of creative expression.

Selecting the right notebook

The notebook you choose for your creative journal depends on your purpose and the type(s) of media you intend to apply to it. For example, if you want to use acrylic paints or watercolors, you want a notebook that has paper thick enough to handle the media.

TIP

For creative journals, I recommend using artists notebooks, in sizes ranging from 6-x-9 inches to 9-x-12 inches, because they're large enough to apply a variety of media to and easy to carry.

You can also find notebooks labeled specifically for art or visual journaling. These notebooks usually contain art-weight paper and also sometimes include art journaling prompts or techniques.

Paper thickness or weight is measured in pounds (lb.) or grams per square meter (GSM). As a frame of reference, paper used in offices and home printers is usually around 70 to 80 GSM, and newspaper stock is 30 to 35 lb., which equals 45 to 50 GSM.

Your choice of paper weight depends on the type of media you want to use. Here are my recommended notebook paper weights for each type of media:

>> **Notebooks for colored pencils and markers:** If you're planning to use pens, colored pencils, or markers, look for a spiral bound artist's sketchbook or pad that has 80-lb. (130-GMS) paper. If you get paper that's thinner than 80 lb., colors might bleed through to the other side.

Most notebooks in this range also work well with stickers and pasting photos or magazine images.

>> **Notebooks for pastels, paints, and multimedia:** Look for an artist's notebook that has a minimum paper weight of 140 lb. or 300 GSM.

Art journals that are labeled for multimedia usually contain heavy-enough art stock — but be sure to read the details before purchasing.

Practicing Creative Journaling Methods

In the following sections, I introduce you to some simple creative journaling techniques that you can use in your creative journal going forward.

To begin, you need only this book, your pen or pencil, and a set of coloring pens, crayons, pencils, or markers.

While you play with these exercises, know your reason for wanting to express yourself creatively, let go of the results, and have fun.

Although I provide creative journaling examples of the exercises, when you're responding to the prompts, don't try to copy the examples. Go ahead and use them for reference, but let you be you — even if that means changing the directions or the prompts.

Writing in shapes

This simple and fun exercise involves creating shapes and then writing your thoughts and feelings using the shapes as guides.

Do This

Follow these steps:

1. **Choose a writing tool of any color.**

2. **In the space provided at the end of this list, draw two or three large, simple shapes, such as rectangles, circles, and triangles.**

   Choose a color that reflects your mood or, just for fun, use a different color for each shape.

3. **Using your pen or pencil reserved for writing, write in words along the contours of the shapes your reasons for wanting to try creative journaling.**

   If writing about your reasons for journaling doesn't appeal to you, write about something you enjoyed doing today or anything else that inspires you.

4. **Doodle or color in some of the shapes.**

   You can also fill in space on the page with color.

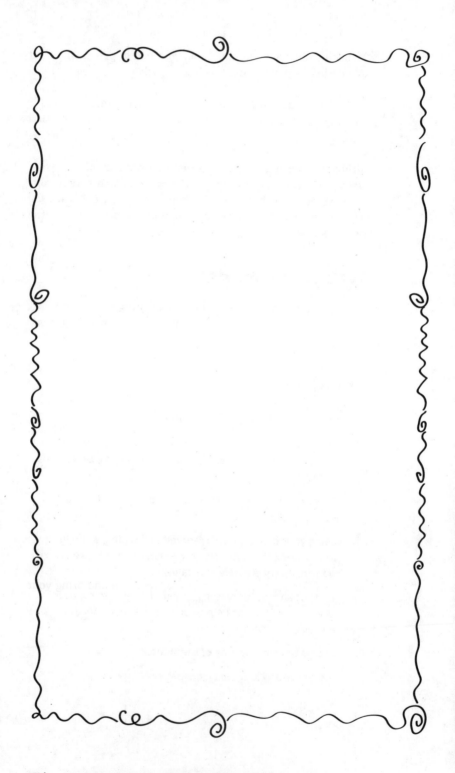

As you can see in the example in Figure 8-1, you don't need any special drawing skills. Don't worry about whether your results have artistic merit. Have fun with colors and shapes, blended with writing, and see where it leads you.

FIGURE 8-1: Writing in and around shapes.

Doodling with color

Doodling with color is a creative journaling technique that has a meditative quality to it that can slow you down and bring your awareness to the present moment.

Do This

Just follow these steps:

1. **Fill a blank page with doodles.**

   Doodling, by definition, is an absent-minded form of scribbling or drawing. So you don't need to have any ideas or themes in mind when you start. Simply draw a few lines or circles and then build on them. While the doodle begins to take shape, you might get an idea about how to expand it. Or not. Let whatever happens, happen.

2. **Add color to the doodles.**

3. **(Optional) If you want, add words in and around the doodles about how you feel in this moment.**

   You can also write about something the doodle may have reminded you of or inspired you to think about.

See an example of this exercise in Figure 8-2. I used a colored ballpoint pen and colored pencils. When I started this doodle, I was feeling somewhat stressed and had no idea what I would draw. When I was done, I realized I felt calm and relaxed, and the doodle (including the strange little gnome) reminded me of the time I enjoyed earlier that day in my garden.

FIGURE 8-2: Doodling on a creative journal page.

Coloring outside the lines

This exercise is intended to release some of your inner childlike play and free self-expression by tapping into unstructured scribbling and spontaneous inspiration.

Do This

Follow these steps:

1. **Fill an entire page with scribbled color.**

   You can use one or any combination of colors. (I used bright purple, yellow, and blue crayons.)

2. **Open a dictionary or book, close your eyes, and point at the page.**

3. **Open your eyes and find the word your finger is touching — that's the word you'll use for your journaling prompt.**

4. **Write your word in big letters anywhere you want on the page.**

   You can write it in the middle, the top, or the bottom of the page; diagonally across the page; or sideways along one edge of the page. You can use decorative or plain lettering.

   I landed on the word *safe,* so I wrote it in the center of my journal page; see Figure 8-3.

5. **Draw shapes or symbols that represent the word.**

   For my example, I drew an umbrella because it symbolizes being covered and safe to me.

6. **(Optional) Brainstorm other words and images that you associate with the first word.**

   I added words such as *protected* and *happy* because these are the feelings I associate with feeling safe.

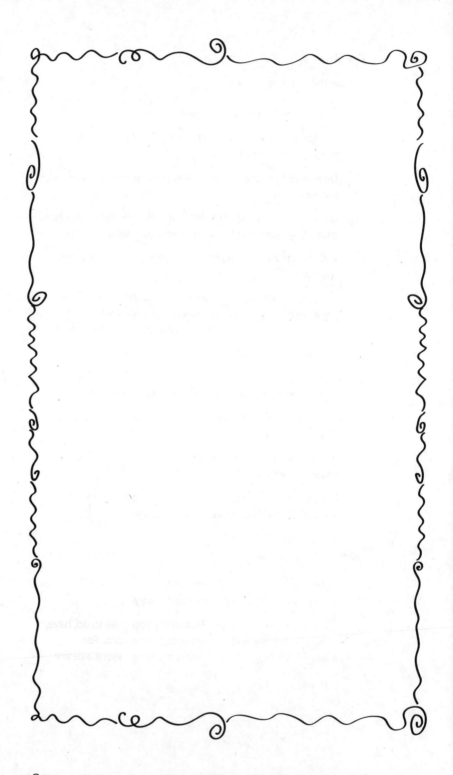

FIGURE 8-3:
An example
of the
"Coloring
outside the
lines"
exercise
using
crayons and
ink pen.

Exploring multimedia

The purpose of this exercise is to begin expanding your toolkit beyond the use of writing and coloring.

Before beginning, gather your supplies: In addition to writing utensils (choose any combination of pens or pencils in a variety of colors), you need glue and/or double-sided sticky tape, and some old photos and/or magazine pages that you don't mind cutting.

TIP

If you want to use personal photos for this activity, consider using your own creative journal notebook instead of the space provided in this book.

Do This

Follow these steps:

1. **Using old photos and/or magazine pictures, cut out images that appeal to you in some way.**

The pictures can represent something you'd like to do, have, or be. Or they can evoke memories or emotions. For example, a picture of a mountain might represent a desire to reach a particular goal. Or a person in a photo might remind you of a particular memory.

Cut out as many images as you want and that will fit in the space provided. (If you prefer to use your own journal notebook, you can cut enough images to fit on either one page or a page spread.)

2. **Paste the pictures to the page.**

   Arrange the pictures in any way that feels good to you and expresses what the images say or mean to you.

3. **Doodle on top of and around the pictures to help express their meaning to you.**

   Play with colors, shapes, and lines that add to your intended expression for the journal entry — or that simply add color and aesthetic appeal for you. Perhaps a sense of whimsy.

4. **(Optional) Add writing, if you want.**

   Add any words that make your journal entry more meaningful to you. For example, to add to the idea in Step 1 of a mountain picture representing achieving a goal, you could write the name of the goal along the side or up the mountain.

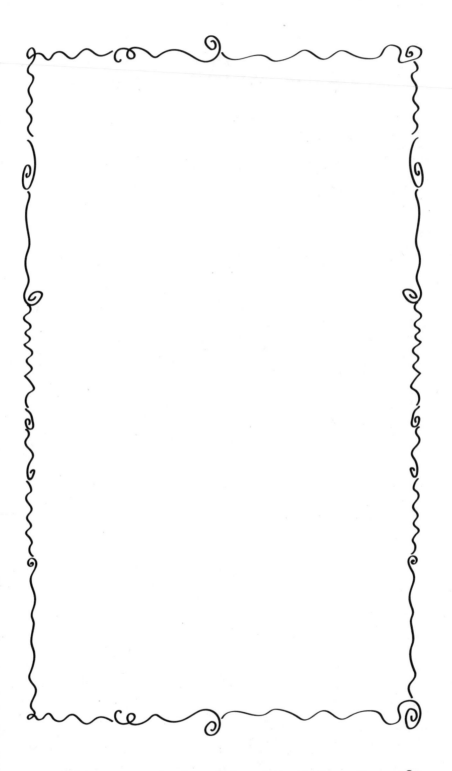

STAYING IN THE CREATIVE ZONE WITH PLAY-INSPIRING PROMPTS

Here are a few creative journaling prompts to help you keep your creative juices flowing:

- Create a journal page about a destination that you want to visit.

- Draw or paint a self-portrait in caricature. Color it with shades that match today's mood.

- Fill a page with drawings or paste pictures of objects you love.

- Go for a walk and collect small flowers, leaves, or bits of decorative grass. Use the items to create a page about your walk.

- Cut out pictures from magazines of people whom you wish you could meet. Paste those pictures to a new journal page. Doodle over and around them.

- Express your present mood using only colors, lines, and shapes.

- Think about a favorite game that you played as a child and journal about it visually.

Chapter **9**

Improving Life with Gratitude Journaling

G ratitude journaling is the practice of writing down the things you're grateful for. It's a way of continually reminding yourself, no matter what else is going on, of what's going well in your life and of the good that continues to come your way.

The difference between gratitude journaling and other forms of journaling is gratitude journaling's narrow focus. For instance, reflective journaling (which I talk about in Chapter 5) is designed to help you think deeply about and find meaning in your life, and Bullet Journaling (flip back to Chapter 7) is a system of organization and reflection about goals, tasks, and events. Although these other types of journaling may include incidentally writing about things you're grateful for, gratitude journaling is the only type of journaling that is focused solely on noticing and acknowledging the positive in your life.

In this chapter, you can explore what keeping a gratitude journal means for you and how you can benefit from it. You can delve deeply into the concept of gratitude and figure out how to practice this type of journaling by using simple prompts.

Defining What Gratitude Means to You

The word *gratitude* comes from the Latin word *gratus*, which means "pleasing" or "thankful." Synonyms for gratitude include appreciation, gratefulness, thankfulness, thanks, recognition, and acknowledgment.

On its face, gratitude seems like a simple concept: being thankful for the good things in your life. But gratitude can be surprisingly difficult to define. Is it a feeling or a way of seeing the world? Is being grateful a personality trait or a developed attitude? Like most concepts, gratitude — what it is and how it's communicated — can mean different things to different people.

What does being grateful mean to you? Take a moment to define it for yourself and include what happens for you mentally and emotionally when you feel and express gratitude. For example, when you're grateful do you feel happy, contemplative, or open? Do you feel more or less expressive? And what are some of the ways you express gratitude?

Do This

Complete the following sentences:

When I am grateful, I feel _____

_____

_____

_____

I express my gratitude by _____

_____

_____

_____

Giving Thanks: Experiencing the Benefits of Gratitude

TIP

Gratitude journaling is so beneficial that, of all the forms of journaling, it tends to have the most impact for the least amount of effort. For this reason, I highly recommend adding gratitude journaling to your regular writing practice as often as possible.

Because gratitude journaling is a focused form of mindfulness (Chapter 6 provides an in-depth look at mindful journaling), it has many of the same benefits of mindful journaling, including increasing your overall health and sense of well-being. Yet there are additional ways that practicing gratitude and, in turn, gratitude journaling can improve your life.

Lowering your stress levels

Work, home, relationship, and financial pressures can quickly add up to a challenging — and stress-filled — life. And, although limited amounts of stress can help spur you to achieve more or perform better, too much stress stimulates the body's fight-or-flight response, raising your heart rate along with your anxiety level. Experiencing this kind of stress over a prolonged period of time can result in health issues ranging from headaches, fatigue, and irritability to depression, high blood pressure, and heart disease.

Fortunately, practicing gratitude can alleviate stress by decreasing its negative affect, increasing an overall sense of well-being, and strengthening strategies for coping with life's challenges.

Do This

Follow these steps to use gratitude to lower your feelings of worry and stress.

1. **Think about someone or something in your life that's currently causing you stress or feelings of anxiety.**

2. **Rate that stress on a scale from 1 to 5.**

   In this scale, 1 is low stress and 5 is high.

3. **In the space provided, write down as least one thing about that person or situation that you can be thankful for.**

   It's okay if you have to work at finding something positive.

   For example, if I'm feeling anxious about money, I might write about how thankful I am that I found a great sale on meat and was able to stock up, or how being tight on money is teaching me to spend more wisely.

   _____

   _____

   _____

   _____

Rate your stress level now, after finding something affirmative to write about the situation or person. Has it shifted a little? Ideally, you feel a bit more optimistic and less stressed after naming at least one thing to be thankful for.

If you aren't experiencing a slight shift toward the positive, or if thinking about the situation or person has actually increased your stress level, don't worry. Try finding additional positive things about the person or situation that you can feel thankful for. Immersing yourself in a feeling of gratitude is almost guaranteed to lower your feelings of worry and stress.

Renewing perspective

When you're in physical or emotional pain, when you've experienced a significant loss or setback, or when life seems like one hard blow after another, it's easy to get mired in dark thoughts and feelings — and it can be extremely difficult to feel grateful.

Establishing a gratitude practice through journaling can provide a path to a higher-level perspective of what's happening. Reminding yourself of the positive things and people in your life has the emotional effect of lifting you up and placing you on a virtual mountain top. From there, the visibility is better, and you can see more clearly.

Do This

Gratitude empowers you to see your pain with a renewed perspective and to find the gifts in your losses.

Try this exercise for renewed perspective:

1. **Think about a period in your life when you experienced a difficult time.**

2. **Looking back now, how did you grow and change from that experience?**

   Or what good came out of that experience? (You can always find something good if you look hard enough.) In the space provided, write down what you gained or the positive outcome that you came up with.

   One way to see the positive is to ask, "In what ways am I better off for having that experience?" For example, imagine you got a flat tire on the way to a job interview. Because of the flat you had to call and reschedule. Maybe you even lost the job opportunity. Sounds pretty awful, right? But think: In what ways are you better off? Maybe you found another job that you truly enjoy, or perhaps as a result you now make it a habit to leave early for important events just in case you are delayed.

   _____

   _____

   _____

   _____

   _____

   _____

3. **What does finding something positive in a difficult time do to your perspective?**

Write your thoughts about this question in the space provided.

_____

_____

_____

_____

Becoming more self-aware

Gratitude increases your awareness of everyone and everything around you, as well as your relationships to those people or objects. And as a result of becoming more *other-aware*, or more aware of others, you naturally become more self-aware.

It's like identifying where you are on a map by looking at the landmarks around you. After you know where you are, as well as where you are in relationship to everything else, you can move through the world more confidently.

Do This

Use this exercise to become more self-aware:

1. **Right now, right where you are, look around.**

2. **List five objects or people you see on the following lines, skipping a line between each item.**

_____

_____

_____

_____

_____

_____

_____

_____

_____

3. Next to each item or person you list in Step 2, write something you can feel grateful for about it or them.

4. Why do you think you chose those five things out of everything else around you?

What do your choices tell you about yourself? Write your answer in the space provided.

_____

_____

_____

_____

_____

_____

_____

Readjusting your attitude

Do you ever find yourself annoyed by circumstances and others' behaviors that are outside your control? Perhaps you were in a hurry to drive somewhere only to get stopped at every red light along the way, causing you to be late. Or maybe you came home from work exhausted, only to discover a messy house — and really, why can't your teenage kids just pick up after themselves once in a while?

It's both normal and easy to let circumstances push you into a lousy mood and to think the whole day's been bad when one thing goes wrong — even when the rest of the day hasn't been so awful. Everyone gets into a funk sometimes.

By using your gratitude journal, you can raise your emotional state to a more positive level, turning that bad mood right around and, if not eliminating it altogether, at least alleviating it.

As a bonus, if you had a good day, your gratitude journal can help you raise your emotional state to an even higher level.

Do This

Follow these steps to help shift your attitude in a positive direction:

1. **Take stock of how you're feeling right now about your day.**

   Has it been a good day or a bad day?

   Note: If you do this exercise in the morning, reflect on the previous day.

2. **Using the space provided, write down the positive and negative things that you can remember about your day.**

   Use a separate line for each item.

   _____

   _____

   _____

   _____

   _____

   _____

   _____

   _____

   _____

   _____

   _____

3. **Next to each positive item, write something about it that you can be thankful for.**

4. **Next to each negative item, write something about it that you can be thankful for.**

   After completing Steps 3 and 4, how do you feel about your day? Hopefully, bringing gratitude to the forefront has shifted your attitude in a positive direction.

Increasing generosity

One of the benefits of a gratitude journaling practice that you may not expect is increased feelings and behaviors of generosity.

According to Christina Karns, contributing author of *The Gratitude Project: How the Science of Thankfulness Can Rewire Our Brains for Resilience, Optimism, and the Greater Good* (New Harbinger Publications, 2020), practicing gratitude builds neural connections in the brain between thankfulness and altruistic responses. Karns cites multiple studies that demonstrate a correlation between keeping a gratitude journal and an increased response in the reward center of the brain when performing an altruistic act such as donating to charity. (That reward center is also known as the ventromedial prefrontal cortex for our science types.)

In other words, though altruistic acts, by themselves, activate the reward center in your brain, practicing gratitude *increases* that pleasure you feel when you do something to benefit others. And this correlation makes sense: When you feel that you've received a lot, *and* you feel gratitude for that abundance, you are likely to perceive that you have more to give. You may then respond by giving more to others — and boost your feelings of pleasure in the process.

Do This

Try this exercise to help boost your feelings of generosity:

1. **Write down three ways that others have been kind to you or contributed to your life in the last few days that you can be grateful for.**

   Consider services or interactions you might otherwise take for granted: for example, having something delivered to your door, a smile from someone in passing, a pleasant waiter at a restaurant, or a clerk finding something for you at the grocery store.

   _____

   _____

_____

_____

2. **Think of and write down three similar ways you could contribute to people you encounter.**

_____

_____

_____

_____

3. **Perform your own small experiment.**

Review what you're thankful for in Step 1, and then find a way to do one or more of the actions you wrote in Step 2 as soon as possible.

In the following space provided, write what you did and how you felt while you did it. Do you think being grateful for others' actions increased your own sense of satisfaction when giving? Why or why not?

_____

_____

_____

_____

_____

Finding happiness

Keeping a gratitude journal can simply make you happier. People who practice gratitude on a regular basis report feeling more optimistic, better able to deal with life challenges, able to recognize and enjoy good experiences more readily, and build better relationships — all characteristics of happy people.

SCIENCE-BACKED FACTS ABOUT GRATITUDE

Since at least 1998, when *positive psychology* was introduced to the field of psychology by renowned American psychologist Martin Seligman, social scientists have conducted a myriad of studies to understand the subjective and objective effects gratitude has on individuals.

Collectively, their large body of work has uncovered some surprising benefits of gratitude, including

- **Staying healthy:** Gratitude is good for controlling your cholesterol and blood pressure — research shows that people who express gratitude have higher good cholesterol and lower bad cholesterol, as well as lower blood pressure.

- **Taking care of yourself:** People who are grateful for their bodies and their health tend to take better care of themselves and exercise more.

- **Attaining your goals:** It turns out that people who are thankful tend to have more positive energy that leads them to work harder for their what they want.

- **Getting good sleep:** Grateful people get better quality sleep.

- **Reacting to others:** Gratitude increases empathy and decreases aggression.

Gaining a Deeper Understanding of Gratitude

When asked to find something to feel grateful for, it's simple to point out the obvious. For instance, when I put my gratitude on auto-pilot, I'm always grateful for a roof over my head, regular meals, physical health, and hot water — and I truly am grateful for those things. But I may be missing an opportunity to dig a little deeper into recognizing the less obvious gifts and true abundance in my life.

REMEMBER

Gratitude journaling can help you attain a greater understanding of the abundance you have — and therefore a deeper sense of gratitude — by helping you to look more closely at your life and acknowledge all the people and resources that are involved in bringing that abundance to you.

Recognizing what you have

Take stock. Think about all that you have. You don't have to be rich by common definition (meaning have a lot of money) to be rich in other kinds of wealth.

Maybe you're rich in artistic talents or have a wonderful support system of family and friends. Perhaps you've traveled the world and are rich in experiences or are in exceptional health, which is its own precious kind of wealth.

Do This

List as many positive aspects of your life as you can come up with. Think deeply and keep listing beyond the first few items that come to mind. (Use an extra sheet of paper if you run out of space here.)

_____

_____

_____

_____

_____

_____

_____

_____

_____

_____

_____

_____

_____

_____

_____

_____

_____

_____

_____

_____

Did it surprise you, how many things you were able to list?

Acknowledging your sources

In this section, dive even deeper than you did in the preceding section. Look at all the resources used in bringing those positive things and people that you list in that section into your life. Examine the chain of events and people involved.

Do This

This exercise helps you identify and acknowledge the sources of some of the positive things in your life.

1. Select just five of the positive items you listed in the preceding section, "Recognizing what you have," and rewrite them in the following numbered areas.

   Item 1

   _____

   _____

   _____

   _____

_____

_____

Item 2

_____

_____

_____

_____

_____

Item 3

_____

_____

_____

_____

_____

Item 4

_____

_____

_____

_____

_____

Item 5

_____

_____

_____

_____

_____

2. **For each item, go back and write down everything you can about its production, shipping, marketing, and so on, including the people involved.**

For example, if you wrote down *hot water* as something that you're thankful for, list things such as the city water distribution system and all its employees; the people who make and read the water meters; internal plumbing for your house and the plumbers who installed it; natural gas production and transportation; water heater manufacturers and their employees; trucking companies and truckers; safety inspectors; retail and building supply stores and all their employees.

If you wrote down a person's name whom you're thankful for, list the factors contributing to that person coming into your life: their parents; how their family immigrated to your country, if applicable; where you met; other people involved, including doctors that brought them into the world, the medical care they've received, and those who've positively influenced that person.

When you begin to examine the details and sources of the many gifts in your life, your sense of gratitude expands to include all those factors.

Appreciating abundance

The Merriam-Webster dictionary defines *abundance* as 1) an ample quantity; 2) affluence, wealth; and 3) a relative degree of plentifulness.

REMEMBER

Your ability to appreciate abundance is in direct proportion to your ability to recognize and acknowledge the good things and people in your life. Keeping a gratitude journal empowers you to do just that.

No matter who you are, what you have or don't have, whether your life is easy or hard, when you begin exploring gratitude, the relative abundance of life, family, and belongings you enjoy becomes more apparent to you.

TIP

If you struggle to see abundance in your life, start by looking to nature — the unending universe, the plentiful air and light. Look to the abundance of life experiences you have had and all the ways they have helped you grow as a person.

Practicing Simple Gratitude

Like with any new practice, start small when you begin gratitude journaling. You can do it in only a few minutes a day by using simple, focused prompts. The benefit of these types of prompts is that they help you center quickly on specific areas of your life.

Doing it daily

Incorporating gratitude journaling on a daily basis for three to six weeks is the best way to make it a habit. After you establish it as part of your regular journaling practice, reassess and decide whether you want to continue doing it daily or on some other regular schedule, such as weekly.

WARNING

Daily gratitude practice can quickly start feeling like a chore if you don't do it with presence and intention. To avoid taking your gratitude for granted, use a different prompt every day.

The following list provides some simple, focused prompts that you can use on a rotating basis to keep your daily gratitude practice feeling fresh and alive.

Do This

Each day, for the next seven days, select one of the following prompts and respond to it in your journal. You can write about

>> Five things that you're thankful for in this moment.

>> A simple daily pleasure that gives you joy.

>> Who you're most grateful for in your life, and all the reasons you're grateful for that person.

>> An appliance that makes your life easier. What is it, and why are you grateful for it?

>> What you're thankful for in your work.

>> The ways you're grateful for your family.

>> A mentor or teacher whom you feel grateful for.

>> Skills or talents that you possess that you're thankful for.

>> Five to ten things in the space near you right now that you're grateful for.

>> Twenty-five reasons you're happy to be alive.

You can do daily gratitude journaling on its own or incorporate it into any other type of journaling that you like to do.

Starting with yourself: Showing your body gratitude

Many people find it difficult to feel and express gratitude for their bodies, because it's easier to judge themselves negatively and focus on their flaws. If this situation is true for you, you may benefit by including body gratitude in your gratitude journaling practice.

Although most developed countries have come a long way, culturally speaking, toward accepting a variety of body types, there's still a great deal of pressure to look a particular way or have a particular shape. As a result, it can be hard to look in the mirror and feel good about yourself in comparison to those idealized bodies. Yet the idealized body is a myth. And the truth is that every person's body is unique.

Body gratitude is about discovering the joy of living in your body. It can help you bridge the gap between a poor body image and feeling positive about your body — *with* all its imperfections — by focusing on being grateful for the *experiences* you have in your body. It's about how you experience life physically — from the inside out, rather than the outside (appearance) in.

Do This

When you pay attention to your body and all the wonderful things that it does and accomplishes in a day, you can begin to appreciate it so much more.

Respond to the following three prompts:

>> Close your eyes and focus on your breathing. Feel the air moving in and out of your lungs.

Take a moment to thank your lungs in writing for literally breathing life into your body.

_____

_____

_____

_____

>> Focus on your hands. Look at your palms, your fingers, the backs of your hands. Wiggle your fingers. Clench your fists and open them again. Think about all the things your hands do during a normal day.

Write about what you're grateful for about your hands.

_____

_____

_____

_____

>> Focus on your legs. Stand up and feel how they support you. Squat or bend your knees. Walk around. Feel how your thighs and hamstrings work.

Sit and write about what you're grateful for about your legs.

_____

_____

_____

_____

How do you feel about your body after writing to the prompts?

_____

_____

REMEMBER

Appreciating how your body works, how it supports you, and the experiences you have in your body naturally increases the gratitude you feel for it. And that, in turn, can improve your overall feelings of body confidence and positivity.

Make a list of all the ways you enjoy your body and all the things your five senses enjoy. Use your list as prompts for your body-gratitude journaling practice.

_____

_____

_____

_____

_____

_____

_____

_____

_____

_____

_____

Practicing Uncommon Gratitude

Uncommon gratitude is a deep, meaningful form of thankfulness in which you identify and acknowledge the positive in all aspects of your life. With uncommon gratitude, you go beyond surface-level appreciation by finding something to be thankful about in every object, situation, event, and relationship — _especially_ those that are typically seen as negative or painful.

Let me be clear that expressing simple gratitude for the obvious good things in your life can bring about all the benefits discussed in this chapter. However, by using your gratitude journal to practice uncommon gratitude — regularly challenging yourself to discover and record the positive in *all* your experiences — you will build a stronger foundation for an optimistic attitude toward life.

Flip the script: Reconsidering the terms you use

Start by questioning your assumptions about what's good and what's bad. *Good* and *bad* are both judgment words that determine something's worth or moral standing. In comparison, terms such as *pleasant* and *unpleasant*, or *wanted* and *unwanted*, are more accurate when applied to life experiences because they express a subjective perspective. And subjective perspectives can be shifted.

Think about it. If you say someone is a *bad person*, you're judging their character as though it's an absolute part of who they are and not possible to change. On the other hand, if you say someone is being *unpleasant*, you're expressing your perspective about their behavior, not their innate character.

The same concept is true of situations in which you find yourself: When you call a circumstance a *bad* situation, it feels dire; an *unwanted* situation feels manageable, and the term implies that you have the ability to do something about it.

TIP

When you begin examining the ways in which you express your gratitude, these simple shifts in terminology can help open your mind and heart to finding the positive in every life experience.

Do This

In this exercise, you can sort the different things, situations, people, and relationships in your life into two categories: Wanted and Unwanted.

When you write about the Wanted parts of your life, include all the things it's easy to feel grateful for, such as health, close friends, loving family, a comfortable home, and simple pleasures such as hot baths and coffee in the morning.

When you write about the Unwanted parts of your life, include difficult relationships, mechanical failures you're having to deal with, inconveniences, annoyances, items you wish you didn't own, and so on.

Go ahead and write down as many things you can think of for each category in the space provided.

Wanted

_____

_____

_____

_____

_____

_____

_____

_____

_____

_____

_____

_____

_____

_____

_____

_____

Unwanted

_____

_____

_____

_____

_____

_____

_____

_____

_____

_____

_____

_____

_____

_____

Review what you wrote in each category and consider how thinking about the items as Wanted or Unwanted, rather than Good or Bad, changes your perceptions of them. Note your findings here.

_____

_____

_____

_____

_____

_____

Embracing the unwanted

The hardest part of practicing uncommon gratitude is finding something to be grateful about that unwanted thing or person that has come into your life.

Whenever you find yourself complaining about someone or something, recognize that you have an opportunity to use your gratitude journal to change your perspective and, ultimately, your response to whatever is happening. Through your journaling practice, you can transform the unwanted into a gift.

Do This

Use this series of prompts whenever you find yourself in an undesirable situation. For the purposes of this exercise, think of something currently in your life that you find painful or annoying.

1. **Write down in the space provided a description of whatever it is you're experiencing that you don't want.**

    Example: *I have insomnia and am only averaging four hours of sleep at night.*

    _____

    _____

2. **If there are any parts of this experience or situation that you have the power to change, write down what you're thankful about being able to change in the space after Step 3.**

    Example: *I am thankful I've found that practicing yoga and drinking chamomile tea in the evenings can sometimes help.*

3. **If you don't see any ways that you can change this experience or situation, write down in the space provided what you can be thankful for in *spite* of not being able to change it.**

    Example: *I'm thankful I have a job with flexible hours so I can take naps during the day.*

    _____

    _____

    _____

    _____

4. **Write about the supportive people in your life in the space provided.**

    How are they helping you, and how can you express your thankfulness to them?

Example: *My partner has been great about providing a calm environment before bed at night and being understanding when I get cranky from lack of sleep. I can express my thanks more by telling him how much I appreciate him, giving him a card, or buying him a small gift.*

_____

_____

_____

_____

5. **What can you be grateful for finding out about yourself in this situation? Write your answer in the space provided.**

Example: *I'm grateful that I'm managing to cope well with my lack of sleep and allowing myself to get help. I've also become more compassionate towards others who experience health issues.*

_____

_____

_____

_____

Although making an effort to find things you can be grateful for within an unwanted situation can't solve the situation or make it go away, uncommon gratitude can help you become more resilient, improve your self-awareness and confidence, and be willing and ready to make changes as needed to improve your life.

Bringing uncommon gratitude to life

Beyond finding gratitude in uncomfortable situations (as discussed in the preceding section), uncommon gratitude can give you motivation to express that gratitude in your life and relationships with others — and to spread thankfulness in the form of kindness.

To expand your uncommon gratitude practice, select one of the following prompts and respond to it in your journal. After you write your response, take action based on what you wrote.

Choose one of these prompts each week until you've responded to all of them.

>> **Think about the worst time in your life.** List five things that are better in your life now as a result of what you experienced in that time. How can you share what you discovered with others?

>> **Write down the name of a person whom you take for granted.** Write down three positive traits of that person and then write three ways you could express more appreciation for them.

>> **What are you most grateful about having accomplished?** Can you use that accomplishment to help someone else? If so, how?

>> **Name three people who have helped you become a stronger person.** Write them thank you letters.

>> **List five things you love about your relationship with the person closest to you.** Now, write five ways you could show them that you're grateful to have them in your life. Pick one and do it.

>> **Write down seven ways that you like to be kind to others.** Do one of these kind acts for someone each day for a week.

3

Journaling Your Way to Health and Happiness

Apply a variety of journaling techniques and prompts to assist with the healing of emotional wounds.

Play with methods to uncover and build your creative and problem-solving skills.

Use journaling to succeed by establishing and achieving your goals.

Find your life mission and purpose, and connect with your spiritual side, using your journal as a mirror.

Journal your way through grief by using prompts to help you navigate its challenging emotions and stages.

Enhance all your relationships through journaling — including the one with yourself.

IN THIS CHAPTER

» **Figuring out whether you're ready to journal about trauma**

» **Approaching your trauma from an angle**

» **Uncovering purpose in your pain**

» **Navigating pain and letting it go**

» **Enhancing self-love**

Chapter **10**

Healing Emotional Wounds

D o you feel weighed down or experience emotional pain because of things that happened in your past? Although the distance of time can remove us from the immediate impact of a loss or a traumatic event and even dull the pain, contrary to the common saying, time itself does not heal all wounds.

In this chapter, I provide journaling prompts and exercises that can help you begin writing about trauma, process your emotions, make meaning of what happened, release your pain, and figure out how to love and take care of yourself.

HOW JOURNALING HELPS YOU HEAL

Although emotional healing is complex and there's no magic formula that can give you instant results, journaling has been proven to support the healing process.

According to James W Pennebaker, PhD, one of the leading researchers and a well-known authority on how writing affects healing, "The act of writing about traumatic experience for as little as 15 or 20 minutes a day for three or four days can produce measurable changes in physical and mental health. . . . Indeed, when we put our traumatic experiences into words, we tend to become less concerned with the emotional events that have been weighing us down."

Assessing Your Readiness to Journal About Trauma

When writing about trauma, simply figuring out how to begin can feel intimidating or scary. If you've tried writing about a traumatic event before and writing didn't help, it's possible that you simply weren't ready to face and process your emotions. Although time may not heal our wounds, it can give us enough emotional distance to be able to approach and examine what happened with a fresh perspective.

Before continuing, perform a readiness self-assessment by asking yourself these questions:

>> Do my emotional wounds feel less raw and sensitive than they used to?

>> Can I think about what happened without feeling completely overwhelmed or panicked?

>> Do I feel ready to talk about what happened?

You get the most benefit from journaling if you can answer yes to all three questions. If you answered no to one or more of the questions, consider journaling in combination with professional therapy to help you move forward in the healing process.

TIP

Keep the following advice in mind while you begin journaling about trauma:

>> Start slowly — or at a slant, as described in the following section.

>> Be patient, compassionate, and gentle with yourself. Writing about painful events isn't easy.

>> Stop writing whenever you need to and come back to it when you feel prepared; don't push through the process because forcing yourself when you're not ready can aggravate your wounds.

>> If writing makes you feel worse, you might not be ready yet. Give yourself more time.

>> Consider working with a mental health professional.

Approaching Trauma Indirectly

In her poem, "Tell all the truth but tell it slant," Emily Dickinson argued that instead of overwhelming someone with a harsh truth, it's better to soften the blow by coming at it from an angle. In the same way, when you're beginning to write about a traumatic event or time in your life, it can be easier emotionally to approach it from the side or an angle (a slant) rather than head on.

The prompts in the following sections can help you begin writing about what happened and processing your emotions by considering the trauma indirectly.

REMEMBER

You're writing only for yourself, so write honestly and from your heart.

Get some distance: Writing in third person

Writing in third person is a powerful journaling technique that provides emotional distance from traumatic events. It softens emotional intensity and enables you to explore your trauma more objectively, potentially gaining new insights along the way.

Do This

Write about a traumatic event in the third person, as though it's a story that happened to someone else. Include how this other person (meaning you) responded and how the event affected them.

_____

_____

_____

_____

_____

_____

Read your third-person story back to yourself — out loud, if possible. How does reading about the event as if it happened to someone else change your perspective? For example, did you find that you could include more details about the event? Did you feel more compassion and empathy for the person in your story than you have for yourself? Did you receive any new insights about the event?

Reflect on your answers and then write your thoughts and insights from this exercise in the space provided.

_____

_____

_____

_____

_____

_____

_____

_____

_____

_____

_____

_____

_____

Creative clustering: Pulling from your subconscious

Creative clustering is a process that allows you to associate images, thoughts, and feelings to concepts. When journaling about painful feelings, clustering can help you explore your feelings more deeply by pulling associations and images from your subconscious. At the same time, it gives you emotional and mental space from the event at the source of those emotions.

Here are the general instructions for creative clustering. Specific instructions for using creative clustering for healing follow after this overview.

1. **Write a word or phrase in the center of a blank page and circle it.**

This word is the nucleus of your cluster. (A *nucleus* is something at the core or center and is the most important part of an object or concept.)

2. **Write whatever associated words come to mind.**

Let the writing radiate outward from the center.

3. **Draw a circle around each word or phrase.**

Don't think too long or analyze, just keep letting those associations flow.

4. **Continue writing associations and ideas triggered by your nucleus for a minute or two.**

At some point, you may feel an urge to write. You might feel this urge as a desire to clarify your thinking.

5. **When you feel this urge to write, take a moment to scan your clustered words.**

6. **When a sentence or the beginning of a sentence comes to mind, start writing.**

Continue writing for a few minutes, or until you feel done. You don't have to use all the words or concepts in your cluster.

See Figure 10-1 for an example of a creative cluster.

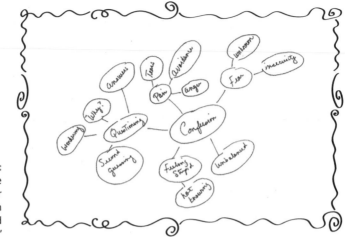

FIGURE 10-1:
A creative cluster starting with the word "confusion."

Do This

To begin your creative cluster, follow these steps:

1. **Take a few deep, slow breaths to calm and bring yourself into the present moment.**

2. **Identify the main feeling that comes up for you about the traumatic event and write it in the center of your cluster in the space provided.**

   Is that feeling sadness, regret, depression, anger, or something else? Make this feeling your nucleus word.

3. **Write down the next word that comes to mind.**

4. **Circle the new word and draw a line from the nucleus to it.**

5. **Focus on the nucleus word again and keep jotting down associated words, circling them, and drawing a line to link the words together.**

   Allow the associated words to spiral outward. For example, in nearby Figure 10-1, the word "pain" is associated to the nucleus word, and "fear" has the words "tears," "avoidance," and "anger" associated with it.

Don't think too much or analyze — simply record words and images when they bubble up.

REMEMBER

When you have completed your cluster, review the words you wrote down. What do you notice? Were some words, emotions, or images repeated? Did the mood or emotion shift? How do you feel in this moment? Can you gain any insights from what you wrote?

Spend a few minutes journaling about what you noticed and any new understanding you gained from this process.

_____

_____

_____

_____

_____

_____

_____

_____

_____

_____

_____

_____

_____

Finding Meaning in Your Pain

One obstacle to healing from trauma or loss is the sense of meaninglessness that often attaches itself to the event. You want to know *why* something happened. You want to understand it because without meaning, you can't find resolution. And in order to heal, you need to find resolution of some kind.

The prompts in the following sections can help you take control of and identify the growth you've gained from — or in spite of — a painful experience. Journaling about how difficulties have impacted you positively, as well as negatively, can help you recognize your strengths and give you a greater sense of purpose. For each prompt, allow yourself to write whatever comes up for you and follow your thoughts to their natural conclusion.

Take control: Changing how you respond

Although you can't change what happened in the past or control others' behaviors, you can use reflective journaling to help control how you respond to what's happening in your life today. (To discover how reflective journaling works, flip to Chapter 5.)

Do This

Think about a specific painful event or issue that makes you feel vulnerable or that makes you wonder, *Why did this happen? Why me?* Write about the ways this traumatic issue or event has influenced your life — your work, family, personal relationships, health, living situation, and so on.

_____

_____

_____

_____

_____

_____

_____

_____

_____

_____

_____

For each of the areas you identified as influenced by the event, journal about the positive ways you could control your responses and activities today and in the future.

_____

_____

_____

_____

_____

_____

_____

_____

_____

Flip the coin: Finding strength in weakness

Experiencing a painful loss or trauma may leave you feeling weak or vulnerable, and you can easily lose self-confidence in these situations. In this exercise, you use journaling to *flip the coin*, switching your internal narrative so that you recognize and acknowledge the strengths embedded in your perceived weaknesses.

Do This

Thinking about a specific loss or event, in what ways do you feel that it made you vulnerable or weak? Write these ways down in the space provided. For example, I might judge myself as having become overly cautious or emotionally reactive.

Because of what happened, I see myself as weak in the following ways: _____

_____

_____

_____

_____

_____

_____

_____

_____

Now, flip the coin: How are your weaknesses also strengths? For example, if I wrote down that I'm overly cautious, I can ask myself how caution is also a strength or positive trait. Being cautious means that I think before acting, I'm careful, and I research and listen to others before making decisions — all positive aspects of caution.

These weaknesses are also strengths because _____

_____

_____

_____

_____

_____

_____

_____

_____

_____

_____

See the good: Shifting your focus

When experiencing a loss or trauma, it's normal to focus on the painful and negative aspects of what happened and find it difficult to see anything positive. However, shifting your focus to the positive things that occurred during or as a result of the event, and expressing gratitude, can elevate your emotions and promote psychological and emotional healing.

Do This

Journal about anything positive that occurred after or during a painful event: Who helped you, what resources were offered to you, and/or how might it have been worse? List 10 things you can be grateful for related to what happened.

_____

_____

_____

_____

_____

_____

_____

_____

_____

_____

Writing Through Pain

You have probably heard the aphorism, "The only way out is through." Sir Winston Churchill said it another way: "If you are going through hell, keep going." It's a truth most of us don't want to hear. Going through a painful situation is like giving birth — once labor has begun, the only way is forward.

If you want to understand and heal the pain you're experiencing, you must be willing to face and, if possible, even embrace painful memories of traumatic events, including difficult relationships, poverty, abuse, and shame. You must be willing to walk directly into your own darkness with a desire to be transformed.

Journaling is an effective — but not easy — way to face that darkness. Pain avoidance is natural and reasonable. On many occasions, I've sat down to write about something difficult in my own life and found myself circling the topic, only managing to pick at the edges of my wound. And you know what? That's okay.

REMEMBER

It's extremely important to be patient with and kind to yourself through this process. There's no "should" — there's only "what is." Accept where you are, be gentle with yourself, and approach the following exercises with curiosity and self-compassion.

WARNING

A word of caution — assess whether you feel ready to face your pain by reviewing the questions in the section "Assessing Your Readiness to Journal About Trauma," earlier in this chapter. If approaching your pain head-on induces additional trauma or triggers panic, you may need more time before you can address it directly. Or you may need professional assistance. There's nothing wrong with either approach.

When you feel ready, use the following prompts to explore what you went or are going through. If you want to respond to all of the prompts, allow some space of time (at least a day) between each journaling session. Confronting too much pain at one time can be overwhelming and emotionally exhausting, causing more harm than benefit for you.

Express your pain

Sometimes, words by themselves can't express feelings adequately. The following creative journaling prompt allows you to express your pain visually and non-verbally, which can aid the healing process. (See Chapter 8 for an in-depth discussion of the creative journaling technique.)

Do This

Using your choice of colored pencils, crayons, or pens, create an abstract drawing in the space provided. Include shapes and colors that express your painful feelings. If you want to, write and/or cut and paste words from a magazine or other source.

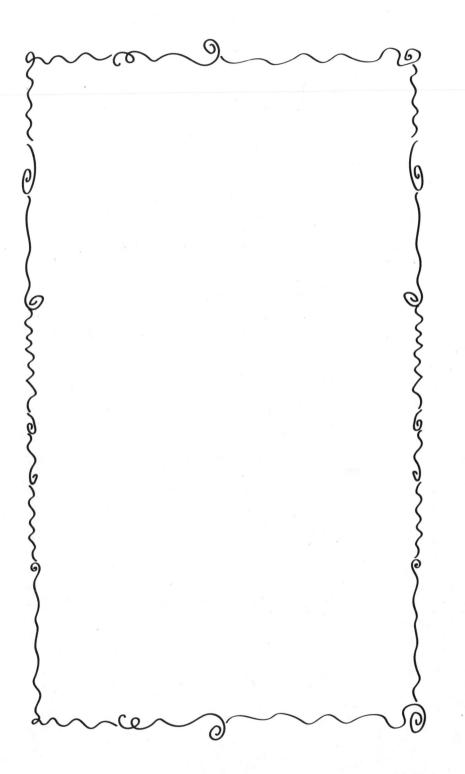

Validate your pain

Pain and its associated feelings — sadness, depression, anger — are usually thought of as negative emotions. Feelings you're not "supposed" to have or that you should just "get over" after an undefined amount of time. Because of these negative associations and because these feelings are, well, painful, it's natural to try to avoid or even deny them.

REMEMBER

The fact is, feelings aren't good or bad. Feelings are simply feelings. They reflect how you respond to and process life, and you have every right to those feelings. You don't have to explain your feelings to anyone, and no one has the right to tell you to feel differently.

Part of the healing process is to acknowledge, validate, and have compassion for your pain. The following reflective journaling prompt can help you start this process (see Chapter 2 to read more about reflective journaling).

Do This

Thinking of a painful experience you're going through now or you have gone through recently, list your feelings and the reasons for feeling the way you do. Be real and don't hold back. Remember, this is your journal, for your eyes only, and nothing you write is wrong.

For example, a person whose best friend just passed away from cancer might write, "I feel angry that I lost Brittany to cancer, and I have every right to feel angry. She was too young to die, and I don't think it's fair or right and I miss her terribly."

Continue naming the different feelings you're experiencing, and remember to validate each feeling, until you feel a sense of completion.

Personify your pain

This creative journaling technique, where you give human traits and characteristics to an abstract concept, animal, or — in this case — emotion is called *personification*. (Go to Chapter 8 for more about creative journaling.) Personifying your emotion can transform your relationship with it and with yourself. This technique effectively allows you to experience your emotion more objectively. When you can visualize and have a conversation with your emotion as something outside yourself, you can establish a cooperative relationship with it — all of which supports the healing process.

Do This

For this journaling exercise, you can use the same painful experience as the one you used in the preceding section or a different experience. Imagine that instead of thinking about your emotion as an abstract concept or a feeling in your body, you picture it as a person. Although this person is strange and you'd rather not have them in your life, they also have positive qualities. What might happen if you took the time to get to know this person and their reason for being in your life?

Step 1: Imagine your emotion as a human-like character

Is your emotion male, female, or neither? Are they tall or short, dark or light? What color are their eyes, hair, and skin? And what kind of clothing do they wear? Give your emotion-person a name and draw a picture or describe what they look like in the space provided.

Step 2: Write a dialogue with your character

Begin a dialogue with your emotion-person by asking why they're present and how they're helping you. Let your imagination take over and allow the conversation to develop naturally.

_____

_____

_____

_____

_____

_____

_____

_____

_____

_____

_____

_____

_____

_____

_____

_____

_____

_____

_____

_____

_____

_____

Step 3: Reflect

What did you discover about yourself or your emotion through your imagined conversation?

_____

_____

_____

_____

_____

_____

_____

_____

Journey to the other side

When you're in the process of healing from a painful event or situation, you can imagine your emotion as a physical landscape. Like personification (see the preceding section), this creative journaling technique (flip to Chapter 8 for in-depth information about creative journaling) helps you gain distance from the raw emotion and a new perspective on your inner journey. As a second step, you can also picture the landscape of your healing destination and look forward to what it might look like, metaphorically.

Do This

To get started, think of your loss or painful event, and then imagine that your feelings are a landscape that you're traveling through. What does that landscape look like? What colors do you see? Is it a wide valley, tall mountain, desert, or body of water? What's the climate like — is it hot or cold, cloudy or bright sky, day or night?

Draw a picture of your landscape.

Next, imagine that you're looking up and forward to the horizon. Describe what you see on the other side of your emotion-landscape — your destination after you make your journey.

_____

_____

_____

_____

_____

_____

_____

What insights or new ideas did picturing your emotional landscape bring to you?

_____

_____

_____

_____

_____

_____

_____

_____

Releasing Your Pain

"Just let it go." You've probably heard that many times. But when it comes to emotional pain, letting go may seem impossible. In part, this is because people think what they're holding onto is a consequence of the circumstance that caused it. In truth, they're holding on because they're afraid of what will happen when they do let go. Will letting go make their loss become permanent and more real? Will letting go mean that justice won't be served?

One of the *Oxford English Dictionary* definitions of the phrase "to let someone or something go" is "to relinquish one's grip on someone or something." Think about that for a minute: Letting go of pain and trauma means relinquishing your grip on it.

What if letting go helped you adjust to life the way it is today? What if letting go meant allowing life to bring you to a new place, maybe a better, truer place that would allow you to thrive?

The following sections can help you consider what letting go of your pain could mean for you personally, understand what's holding you back, and determine what your life might be like if you released your pain.

Determine what "letting go" looks like for you

When you think of letting go of your trauma and pain, what does that inner process look like for you? For example, a person wanting to let go of the pain from losing a home they really loved might begin, "For me, letting go means taking comfort in my good memories but allowing myself to accept a future home that comes my way, even if it's not the same. It means accepting change."

Do This

Free-write about what letting go means to you. (Free-writing is discussed in the Chapter 1.)

For me, letting go means . . . _____

_____

_____

_____

_____

_____

_____

_____

_____

_____

_____

_____

_____

_____

Now, think about what holds you back from releasing your pain. Is it fear that you'll lose memories, or something or someone else, as a result of letting go? After you identify what's holding you back, complete the following prompt.

_____ is preventing me from releasing

my pain, because . . . _____

_____

_____

_____

_____

_____

_____

_____

_____

_____

_____

Make room for something new

You've most likely heard the saying that when one door closes, another opens. Similarly, whenever we let go of something, whether that be something tangible, such as clothing and books, or intangible, such as ideas and emotions, we make room for something new to enter our lives.

Imagining how life might change while you release your pain can help you see how letting go of the object of your emotions could open your life up to something more desirable. How you imagine this (nearly) pain-free world is unique and highly personal.

In the example in the preceding section, for the person who lost their home, they might imagine a move to a new town or finding a completely different type of home altogether. They might imagine a sense of freedom and decide to rent instead of buy or even travel.

Do This

Imagine what it would feel like to release all the emotional pain you've been experiencing — to just let it go and have it float away. Finish the following sentence:

"If I let go of all this pain and trauma, I would have room in my life for . . ."

_____

_____

_____

_____

_____

_____

_____

_____

How do you feel after writing about what you could have room for?

_____

_____

_____

_____

_____

Loving Yourself

Discovering how to love yourself is a critical part of the emotional healing journey.

Loving yourself doesn't mean being selfish or conceited. It means recognizing that your own well-being and happiness are important. It means acting in support of your physical, psychological, and spiritual growth, and not sacrificing your needs to please others. Loving yourself includes accepting who you are, in this moment in time, with all your strengths and weaknesses. It means acknowledging and validating your emotions and giving yourself the kindness that you would want others to extend to you.

In the following sections, use the prompts to help you find out how to love and take care of the most important person in your life: you.

Comfort yourself

Enduring a painful experience or trauma on your own and without the benefit of being comforted by others can increase the resulting feelings of suffering. For example, a child who loses their parent and is then shuffled into the foster system without receiving much-needed comforting in the process is likely to feel more traumatized than a child who was given comfort, compassion, and care. And adults going through painful experiences may be expected to manage or deal with their heartache and left alone to their own devices.

If you have suffered grief or pain without the benefit of being comforted, it's still possible to console yourself as part of the healing process. The following creative journaling prompt allows you to imagine going back in time and comforting yourself. (See Chapter 8 for additional creative journaling ideas.)

Do This

Think about a loss or trauma you experienced in the past and write a letter to yourself — the self that went through that experience. What would you say to comfort the you of the past? Using the knowledge and wisdom you've gained since that event, what advice would you give? Offer your past self the comfort, acceptance, and love that you needed.

_____

_____

_____

_____

_____

_____

_____

_____

_____

_____

_____

_____

_____

_____

Acknowledge yourself

Looking back on some of the difficult times in your life, reflect on the ways those experiences have made you a better person. For example, you might be more compassionate to people in certain situations, feel more resilient, or have gained a sense of purpose. (Flip to Chapter 5 to read how and why reflective journaling works.)

Do This

Write about the strengths and positive attributes you've gained.

_____

_____

_____

_____

_____

_____

_____

_____

_____

_____

_____

_____

_____

_____

_____

_____

_____

_____

Affirm yourself

An *affirmation* is a positive statement that challenges unhealthy and negative thinking patterns. When you speak an affirmation with conviction — that is, when you believe your affirmation — it has the power to push your belief systems in a positive direction. Affirmations can help you feel more positive about yourself and improve self-confidence. So, why not make affirmations a habit?

Do This

Using the strengths you identified in the preceding section, write down five affirmations. For example, if resilience is one of your strengths, you can use the affirmation, "I am resilient."

TIP

Affirmations must be believable to be effective. Check in with yourself after writing an affirmation. In the example I gave, if you don't truly believe you're resilient, the affirmation won't work. In this case, you can change it to, "I want to believe that I'm resilient." This change creates a believable affirmation that can shift your thoughts in the desired direction.

_____

_____

_____

_____

_____

If you say an affirmation once to yourself, it feels good, but the words aren't integrated into how you see yourself and are easily forgotten. To be effective, affirmations need to be repeated on a regular basis, preferably daily. The following activity helps you make a habit of affirming yourself.

Do This

In your journal, create a habit tracker. (Find out more about habit tracking in Chapter 7.) You can use a simple version, as shown in Figure 10-2, for weekly tracking, checking off each day after you accomplish it.

Habit	M	T	W	Th	F	Sa	S
Practice piano							
Journal							
Say affirmations 2x							
Exercise							

FIGURE 10-2: Example of a weekly habit tracker.

Be sure to include a reminder to look yourself in the eyes in the mirror twice each day while saying your affirmations out loud. Track your affirmations for three to four weeks. At the end of each week, check in again with yourself. Do your affirmations feel believable and natural, or do you feel uncomfortable with some of them? Using reflective journaling, write about how you're feeling (see Chapter 5 for more about this type of journaling).

_____

_____

_____

_____

_____

When an affirmation begins to feel integrated, meaning it feels like a fact, let it go and substitute a new one. When an affirmation feels uncomfortable or you're having a difficult time believing it, adjust the wording to make it more believable and try again. Continue to adjust and substitute affirmations, as needed.

Chapter **11**

Unleashing Your Creativity

reativity — the ability to do something in a new way, to find an elegant or novel solution to a problem, resulting in a valuable idea, product, or work — is innate in all humans to varying degrees. Yet creativity can sometimes seem ethereal and out of reach, possessed only by the world's great thinkers, artists, and inventors.

To counter that notion, it's helpful to acknowledge the many ways you creatively navigate life and find innovative work-arounds to everyday problems. Maybe you discovered a new and tasty way to prepare an old recipe or combined just the right words to poetically describe a color. Or perhaps you put together a brand-new outfit by combining pieces of your existing wardrobe in a unique way.

So, even if you've never thought of yourself as creative before, the first step to enhancing your creativity is to acknowledge that you possess it and that you are, in fact, expressing your creativity countless times each day.

The second step is to engage in activities that unleash and expand your natural creativity. The more you exercise your creative muscle, the stronger your creative nature can grow.

The journaling prompts and reflections in this chapter are designed to help you combine, explore, and transform ideas — and can be used with or alongside any journaling method you usually engage in. Approach these journaling activities with curiosity, playfulness, and a sense of exploration. You never know what treasure you can find.

Celebrating Your Creative Traits

Creative people have traits and skills that are *cross-functional*, meaning they can be used in many areas of their lives, not only in artistic forms. Traits, or personality characteristics, commonly possessed by creative people include being curious, open-minded, flexible, detail-oriented, optimistic, and ambitious, just to name a few. These traits allow them to approach problem-solving with a creative mindset.

The journaling prompts in the following subsections are designed to help you recognize your own, unique creative characteristics and figure out how to apply creativity in your daily life.

Identifying your creative characteristics

To begin building your creativity muscle, this reflective journaling activity prompts you to acknowledge the traits, skills, and strengths you already use creatively in your life. (See Chapter 5 for an overview of reflective journaling.)

Do This

Recognizing and acknowledging your creative attributes helps you increase your awareness of your own creative processes and approach future creative tasks with increased confidence.

1. **In the left column of the blank table that follows these instructions, make a list of as many of your strengths and positive attributes you can think of, including personality characteristics, skills, and natural talents.**

TIP

If you have difficulty identifying your positive traits, think about skills and strengths you possess. Are you good at solving math problems or grasping languages? Maybe you're a proficient dancer or a master gardener. What are the traits you possess that helped you develop these skills? Write these traits down in the blank table provided.

2. **In the right column next to each trait, answer the question: How can this characteristic help me be more creative?**

For example, are you a naturally curious person who has a love of learning? If so, your columns for this entry might look like this example:

Trait	How can this trait or characteristic help me be more creative?
Love of learning	I take in information and ideas that I can then use to find creative solutions.

Trait	How can this trait or characteristic help me be more creative?

3. Take time to reflect.

Did you gain any insights about your creative traits and skills through this exercise? Perhaps you discovered a new way of thinking about your traits and skills. Journal about your emotional reactions and thoughts here:

_____

_____

_____

_____

_____

_____

_____

_____

_____

Considering ways to apply your natural creativity

When you can identify and acknowledge the creative traits, abilities, and skills you own, you're better able to consciously apply those attributes to creative challenges.

For example, I identify "love of learning" as a trait that enables me to research and apply new information to solve problems more creatively. Now that I know how this trait helps me be creative, I can consciously apply it to current and future problems. I have confidence that my ability to find information and relevant ideas can help me come up with an innovative solution to a business or personal challenge. Check out Figure 11-1 for a journal entry I created to help me identify and acknowledge one of my creative traits as well as ways to apply this attribute to a creative challenge.

<table>
<tr><td>Trait: Love of learning_____</td></tr>
<tr><td>Problem or creative challenge: I need a personal training plan for a physically demanding bicycling tour I'm participating in, and I don't know where to start. _____</td></tr>
<tr><td>_____</td></tr>
<tr><td>Actions I can take:

Research different types of training plans for touring.
Ask other touring cyclists what they have done.
Consider my schedule and ability level — where can I start?
Using information gathered, draft a personal plan.
Begin plan and revise as needed along the way.</td></tr>
</table>

FIGURE 11-1: Example entry for identifying and applying a creative trait.

Do This

Follow these instructions to create your own entry:

1. In the space provided, write down a trait or skill that helps you be creative.

Select a trait or skill you wrote in response to the previous activity or identify a new one.

2. Think of a creative challenge you have and add it to your entry.

This could be any kind of challenge. For example, a management decision you need to make for work; an essay you want to write; a piece of art you're working on; a space you want to redesign; or a financial puzzle you need to work out.

TIP

If you can't think of a current challenge, try one from your past.

3. Write down actions you can take using your creative trait or skill.

Trait: _____

Problem or creative challenge: _____

_____

Actions I can take: _____

_____

_____

_____

_____

_____

4. Take time to reflect.

Did you gain any additional insights about your selected trait or skill through this exercise? Perhaps you gained some confidence about how to apply it to different situations. Write your emotional reactions and thoughts here:

_____

_____

_____

_____

_____

Picturing Your Creative Side through Drawing

One way to build creativity is through drawing. For the sake of this discussion and the following prompts, I'm lumping doodling, drawing, and sketching into one term — *drawing* — because they achieve similar results when applied to journaling.

If you don't feel comfortable with drawing and/or tend to judge your art as "not very good," you might be tempted to skip the prompts in the following sections. Don't.

REMEMBER

Drawing is for everyone. You don't need to be talented or trained as an artist to gain the benefits to creativity that it offers you.

Because of its meditative nature, drawing can also help you be present in the moment by making you more aware of contrasting light, color, texture, shade, balance, and form.

Other benefits of drawing include

>> Improving memory

>> Reducing anxiety

>> Elevating mood

>> Lowering pain perception

>> Increasing resilience

The creative journaling prompts in the following sections explore ways to enhance your creativity through drawing, but don't be surprised if you find yourself reaping other benefits, as well. (Flip to Chapter 8 for a more in-depth look at creative journaling.)

LIBERATING FINDINGS ABOUT DOODLING

Drawing, in the form of doodling, was found to enhance concentration and information retention in a famous 2009 study conducted by Jackie Andrade, a psychology professor at the University of Plymouth.

Dr. Robert Burns, former director of the Institute for Human Development at the University of Seattle, maintained that doodling also taps into our subconscious thoughts, and the shapes we draw when our mind is otherwise occupied are symbols of unconscious thoughts.

A 2014 study by Gabriela Goldschmidt, design researcher at Israel Institute of Technology, explored how doodling stimulates new ideas and theorized that drawing creates a "dialogue between the mind, the hand . . . and the eyes," which can spark creativity through new perceptions or ways of thinking.

Moreover, in an interview published by CNN in 2013, Sunni Brown, author and well-known visual-thinking guru, states that one of the benefits of drawing is increased creativity because ". . . you're liberating your mind from traditional, linear and linguistic thinking and moving into a more organic thinking space, heightened information processing, heightened information retention, and the ability to view content from a variety of different angles."

Varying your drawing methods

Pick an ordinary object and, in the space provided, illustrate it in three completely different ways. For example, you might sketch a bare outline of the object. Then, for your second method, you might use colors and abstract forms. For your third, you might cut out pieces of paper and construct the object on the page using those pieces of paper. Depicting an object using three separate methods engages your creative mind as well as your sense of play.

Don't worry about whether your illustrations are objectively good or accurately depict the object you choose. That doesn't matter. Approach this exercise with curiosity and playfulness: How different can you make these illustrations?

Add your first drawing here:

Draw or illustrate the same object using a different method here:

Pull out all the stops and redraw (or represent) the same object in yet another way here:

After you complete the three varied drawings, think about how you came up with ideas for your three illustrations. For example, did you decide what to do ahead of time or just begin drawing and let the ideas flow? Continue evaluating your drawings and process by considering how you'd answer the following questions:

>> Was it difficult or easy at first? At any point, did you feel stumped, even if only for a moment? If so, how did you get past that feeling?

>> Which one of the illustration ideas was the most difficult to come up with?

>> What skills or traits do you have that helped you solve this creative problem?

>> How might you apply those same traits or skills to creatively solve other problems?

Journal for a few minutes on what you discovered about your creative process in response to the previous questions, and how that discovery can help you continue to explore and develop your creative side:

_____

_____

_____

_____

_____

_____

_____

_____

_____

_____

_____

_____

_____

Challenging yourself with continuous line drawing

Another way to explore your creative side through drawing is to draw a picture in one continuous line, without lifting your pencil off the paper. This technique helps stimulate creativity because it focuses on the process rather than the end result. It encourages mindful relaxation, hand-eye coordination, and openness to trying something new. See Figure 11-2 for inspiration.

FIGURE 11-2:
A continuous
line drawing
of a chicken,
including
detail of
one wing
and eye.

Adobe Stock Art

Do This

In the space provided, draw a picture of a cat (or other animal of your choice) in one continuous line, without letting your pencil lift from the page. While you draw, pay attention to how you're feeling about the activity, how you react to trying something new, and what techniques you use to keep the pencil on the page.

TIP

You can make your drawing as simple or complex as you want. If you're attempting something like this for the first time, try just drawing the outline of the animal, without details. If you're feeling adventurous, include additional details.

REMEMBER

It's okay if the end result is messy and silly. Focus on the process and employ your creativity to get to the end.

Take time to reflect on the process. How did drawing a picture in a continuous line feel for you? What can you uncover about yourself by reflecting on your emotional responses and thoughts to this process? And finally, how might you transfer what you discover about your creativity to non-artistic types of creative challenges? Use the space provided to journal for a few minutes in response to these questions.

_____

_____

_____

_____

_____

_____

_____

_____

_____

_____

_____

_____

_____

_____

_____

_____

_____

_____

_____

_____

_____

Playing with Ideas: Stimulating Your Imagination

The following sections give you two methods to generate new ideas:

>> **Free word association:** A well-known technique for prompting fresh ideas, word association taps into subconscious connections between ideas. Word association can be done in a list form, as in the following prompt, or in a form called creative clustering, which is covered in Chapter 10.

>> **Flip the challenge:** Take on problem-solving by looking at what you *don't* want to accomplish, rather than what you *do* want. It's a kind of devil's-advocate approach to idea generation that helps you overcome creative blocks by viewing the issue from another perspective.

Both methods stimulate the imagination because they bypass your usual thinking and problem-solving methods, instead tapping into your intuitive and subconscious creativity.

Using free association

Free association is a widely recognized method for creative problem solving. Essentially, it helps you develop new ideas by creating a chain of associated words. You start with one word or idea, and then rapidly write down the next word that comes to mind, and then the next, and the next, and so on. This process helps you be more creative by tapping into your subconscious, stimulating the imagination, and bypassing typical thinking, which is more deliberative and tends to quickly dismiss new ideas.

Do This

Write the word "innovative" on the top line below. Then, write down the first word that pops into your head after "innovative." Continue writing associated words as quickly as possible (it's okay to repeat words) until no more come to mind.

_____

_____

_____

_____

_____

_____

_____

_____

_____

_____

_____

_____

_____

Review your list of words. Notice word repetition, patterns, imagery, and any surprising associations. What does your list reveal to you about ideas surrounding innovation that you didn't consciously know before you performed the free association? For example, maybe you uncovered some subconscious resistance to innovation, or perhaps you associated innovation with a particular art form or industry.

Journal your thoughts and insights here:

_____

_____

_____

_____

_____

_____

_____

Flipping the challenge

Flipping a challenge involves creatively thinking about the *opposite* of what you want to accomplish. This process can surprise you with innovative ideas about how to solve the initial problem. Flipping a challenge can be fun as well!

For example, imagine you want to reconfigure your living room so that it encourages small-group conversations, but you're feeling a bit stumped because your furniture doesn't seem to be the right size and shape. To flip the challenge, you would come up with all the ways you can use your furniture to discourage and even prevent small-group conversations — for example, positioning a sofa to face the TV or fireplace, or removing coffee and side tables.

Do This

Imagine you're planning a party to celebrate an important life event, such as a graduation or anniversary, and you want to make this an especially memorable and enjoyable event for everyone attending. The problem is that you'll have a wide range of personalities in attendance, from extreme extroverts to extreme introverts, including a few who don't even get along very well. How can you ensure that everyone has a good time?

Flip the challenge by thinking about all the ways you could make them have a *terrible* time. What would you need to do to make sure they never wanted to come to one of your parties again? Write it all down — and remember to have fun with this devilish approach!

_____

_____

_____

_____

_____

_____

_____

_____

Reflecting on your ideas for ensuring guests have a terrible time at your party, what surprising or insightful ideas did you come up with that, if you did the opposite, would help ensure that your attendees have a *great* time at your party? Perhaps in your flipped approach you provided only burgers and fries to a mostly health-conscious group and seated your confrontational aunt with your shy sister.

_____

_____

_____

_____

_____

_____

_____

_____

_____

_____

Pushing Limits: Stepping Outside Your Comfort Zone

One thing that can hold you back from expressing creativity is always staying in your comfort zone — that place where you're confident and comfortable in your thinking and ideas and the ways you express yourself. That place where you feel you belong.

Purposefully pushing your limits and stepping beyond your comfort zone is arguably the best way to increase your self-awareness, confidence, and creative skills.

To use a body-building analogy, if you want to build muscle, you need to select weights that are heavy enough to feel strain when performing a prescribed number of repetitions. If you use light weights that are comfortable, you might maintain the muscle you have, but you won't make any gains.

Creativity works the same way — you need to engage in activities that are just outside that old comfort zone and that feel just a little difficult if you want to encourage creative growth.

Do This

Try a little experiment by following these steps:

1. **Clasp your hands together in front of you, with fingers interlaced.**

   Just clasp your hands in the way that comes naturally. Figure 11-3 shows how to interlace your fingers.

Notice which thumb is on top — your left or your right. Or perhaps they're side by side.

2. **Switch your hands so that the thumb and fingers that you put on top in Step 1 are now on the bottom.**

3. **Hold your hands in this new position while observing how you feel.**

   If the second hand position feels weird or causes your heart rate to increase, or you feel an intense urge to unclasp your hands and revert to the previous position, then you're completely normal. You know you're outside your comfort zone whenever you have this reaction to trying something new.

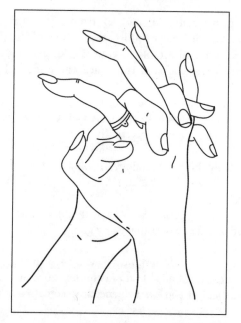

FIGURE 11-3: Hands in the act of clasping, with fingers interlaced.

Adobe Stock Art

The two activities and prompts in the following sections can help you understand your comfort zone boundaries and begin to feel more confident about stepping outside them.

Acting crazy

Behaving in ways that you would not behave normally — being extra silly, singing, dancing, or making noise — is a quick and effective way to practice stepping out of your comfort zone while discovering its boundaries.

For the activity in this section, carefully choose when and where you perform it. Wherever you choose, expect to feel just a little bit uncomfortable or embarrassed while doing the activity. That way, you know you're outside your comfort zone.

If you're the sort of person who's intensely self-conscious, you probably want to do this activity when you're alone. Even alone, you may find this exercise goes outside your comfort zone. However, if you're extroverted and don't mind sometimes acting silly in public (but still feel a little embarrassed), then you might decide to do this activity when there are other people around. (If so, explain what you're doing before you do it so they don't become alarmed.)

Do This

Set a timer for two minutes and start it running. For those two minutes, make spontaneous noise with your body. Claps, slaps, hoots, and hollers. Grunt and groan. Laugh out loud. Stomp your feet. Anything but words. Be prepared — two minutes is going to feel like a *very* long time. While you make these sounds, notice your emotional reactions: Are you having silly fun or judging yourself; do you feel free or restricted?

After the two minutes are up, free-write about your experience with the activity in the space provided. What did it feel like to go so outside of your comfort level? What thoughts did you have while you were making noises? How do you feel now after having done so?

REMEMBER

Going outside your comfort zone is uncomfortable by definition. Identifying and journaling about your comfort zone boundaries can enhance your self-awareness and increase your willingness to go outside self-imposed limits in order to build your creative muscle.

_____

_____

_____

_____

_____

_____

_____

_____

_____

_____

_____

_____

_____

_____

_____

Changing your routine

Do you have the same ritual every morning? How about at night before bed? Maybe your days have a routine rhythm to them that's as cozy as old slippers — safe and comfortable. A great way to stimulate creative growth is by shaking up your routine.

Changing your routine can help you see life and its challenges from a new perspective. Also, as a result of the slight discomfort caused by the change, you become more present in the moment and more alert and engaged in your activity, which in turn stimulates creative thinking.

As an example from my own life, I had the following morning routine after waking: Exercise, then coffee and breakfast, shower, and work. I did this every weekday for years. But I realized that both my exercise and work routines had lost their creative spark, so I decided to switch things up.

I began deciding each night how I wanted to prioritize the next day's activities — while still including exercise, journaling, and my work and household responsibilities. On some days, I'd have my coffee and perform a few gardening tasks before breakfast, and then journal before exercise. On others, I would breakfast, write, then exercise later in the day. Playing with my routine in this way allowed me to experiment and discover new approaches to each activity.

And because I journaled at different times during the day, I found that I was writing about a wider variety of topics and situations, resulting in additional insights and fresh ideas.

Do This

Select a routine that you're open to changing for one week. Next, record how you perform that routine now and how you plan to change its order or method.

I will change my _____ routine for seven days.

Currently, I . . . _____

_____

_____

_____

_____

_____

I will change the routine by . . . _____

_____

_____

_____

_____

_____

After performing the changed routine for one week, reflect on the change's effects. Was making the change easy or difficult? What, if any, perspective changed for you as a result of the changed routine? Did you find new solutions to old problems? Do you plan to keep the change or go back to the way you did things before, and why?

Write your thoughts, insights, and any resulting actions you plan to take in the space provided:

_____

_____

_____

_____

_____

_____

_____

_____

_____

_____

Finding Inspiration from Within

If you most often look to inspiration outside yourself, it's time to discover your natural internal inspiration. You can begin by developing a relationship with your inner muse. In Greek mythology, the muses are goddesses born of Zeus and Mnemosyne, the goddess of Memory, and each presides over inspiration for a different art or science, such as dance, music, and astronomy.

From this mythology springs the idea of a muse as the source of inspiration for any creative endeavor. Your *inner muse*, therefore, is your internal source of creative innovation — born of equal parts imagination, intuition, memory (past experience), and present awareness.

The exercises in the following sections playfully help you find and figure out how to call on your muse at will. Then, whenever you face a creative challenge — whether that's writing, painting, music, or simply figuring out a solution to a difficult problem — you can call on your inner muse (your internal creative resources) for help.

REMEMBER

A brief, humorous note: Muses are notoriously fickle, and although you may develop a great working relationship with yours, they do tend to come and go as they please. Don't feel discouraged if yours doesn't always appear when called.

Getting to know your muse

The first step to working with your muse is getting to know them. After all, how can you call on inspiration without knowing what it looks and feels like and how it works?

Use the following fun prompts to stimulate your imagination, learn how you picture your muse, and prepare for calling on your inspiration when you need.

Do This

How do you picture your muse? What do they look like? For example, is your muse tall or short, have long or short hair, soft or angled features? What type of clothing does your muse wear? Describe in writing or draw how you imagine your muse in the space provided. How you picture your muse reveals a little about how you relate to your intuition. Write about or draw your muse in the space provided.

Describe your muse's personality. What does your muse like and dislike? Are they bold or shy, have a loud or quiet voice, seem nurturing or demanding? What other characteristics do you imagine your muse to have? Like the previous prompt, the characteristics you imaginatively assign to your muse uncovers your attitude toward your intuitive creativity.

_____

_____

_____

_____

_____

_____

_____

Introducing yourself to your muse

The preceding prompts invite you to imagine your muse's appearance and personality characteristics. Getting to know your inner muse (or at least how you perceive them) can help you access your intuitive inspiration by giving it form, even if that form is invented.

Continue this imaginative and playful approach to discovering your inner muse with the following two-part prompt.

Do This

Engage in some pretend letter correspondence with your muse.

1. **Write a short letter to your muse letting them know why you want their help and inviting them to visit you.**

   Describe the creative challenge(s) you're facing and what you hope your muse can provide.

   _____

   _____

   _____

   _____

   _____

   _____

   _____

   _____

   _____

2. **Write a response to your letter from your muse.**

   Imagine how your muse might respond to your request and write the letter from the muse's point of view.

   _____

   _____

   _____

Calling on your muse

After you get an idea of your muse's personality, preferences, and voice (which you can do in the preceding section), you want to develop a personal method for calling on them. Why? Simply because it works!

I've developed my own method, which sets the creative mood for my work while being meditative, ritualistic, and fun. I usually start by lighting a small candle. Then, I close my eyes, breathe deeply and slowly for a few minutes until I feel my heart slow and I am present in the moment. Then, I call my muse with a little mantra that I speak aloud:

> *Dear muse, creative part of my inner being, come sit with me.*
> *Whisper love to me during my creative process, when I am thinking,*
> *imagining, writing. Show me what is possible and feed me gently with*
> *new ideas and expression. Take me to new worlds and inspire me.*

Then I begin my creative work. Although my muse is sometimes shy and makes me wait, in the end, she never disappoints me.

I share my method just to give you one idea of how you might approach your muse. Create your own personal ritual, whatever feels right and natural to you.

Do This

Create your own method for conjuring your muse. How do you want to call on your muse? Journal your ideas in the space provided. Remember to have fun with this exercise, but also make it something you'll actually do.

_____

_____

_____

_____

_____

_____

_____

_____

_____

_____

_____

Chapter **12**

Achieving Success

ike having your own personal life coach, your journal helps you attain the success you want in life by giving you a place to clarify, commit to, measure, and achieve your goals. You can use your journal to identify your desires, skills, and abilities; find your passion; and set a desired direction for your life.

Chapter 7 provides an introduction to goal setting by using the Bullet Journal method. In this chapter, you can explore a variety of different journaling techniques, including reflective (Chapter 5), creative (Chapter 8), and Bullet Journaling, for establishing and tracking progress to achieve what you want in life.

Deciding What Success Means for You

Success means something different for each person. Some people might see success as having a large, luxurious home and enough money to travel internationally as often as they want.

Others might consider themselves successful when they have a strong support group made up of a large circle of loving friends and family. (I read about one couple whose vision of success was to retire and live on cruise ships for the rest of their lives!)

To achieve success in your life, you need to be clear about what it means for *you*. This understanding is the foundation for any goal setting you do and the way you go about achieving those goals. For this reason, your first task while you work through this chapter is to reflect on your perception of success.

REMEMBER

Your definition of success shifts depending on what life stage you're in. When you're young and fresh out of high school or college, success might mean finding the perfect job. A few years later, success might look like providing a safe and stable environment for your young family or establishing a new business. And retirement would look like something else altogether. I recommend revisiting your definition periodically and making changes or adjustments as needed.

Exploring the idea of success

The following reflective journaling prompts help you look at the idea of success from different angles so that you can uncover some of the different ways you think and feel about success.

Do This

Respond to at least three of the following prompts that resonate for you, but feel free to respond to all the prompts when you have the time and inclination.

Prompt 1

Consider someone you know (or know of) whom you consider to be successful. Describe a characteristic or habitual behavior they have that you don't. How would having that characteristic or behavior help you be successful, and how can you incorporate it into your life?

_____

_____

_____

_____

_____

_____

Prompt 2

Rate how important being successful is to you by circling the number that most closely corresponds to how you feel about it.

1	2	3	4	5
Not at all important	Not very important	Neutral/ Don't know	Somewhat important	Extremely important

Journal about why you rated success's importance the way you did? Consider the following questions:

➤ Are your actions in alignment with your rating? For example, if you rated success as highly important, do you take action on a regular basis toward your goals?

➤ What motivates you to succeed?

➤ Compared to how you rated the importance of success, what do you value more — or less — than success?

_____

_____

_____

_____

_____

_____

_____

_____

Prompt 3

If you could have or do or be just *one* thing in this world that would make you feel successful, what would that be, and how would that one thing change your life?

_____

_____

_____

_____

_____

_____

Prompt 4

If you could go back and give your younger self advice about how to live a successful life, what would you say?

_____

_____

_____

_____

_____

List some ways you can follow the advice you gave to your younger self as you go forward in your life.

_____

_____

_____

_____

_____

Prompt 5

Review your answers to the previous prompts in this section. Depending on the prompts you completed, consider the characteristics or behaviors you identified with successful people

(Prompt 1), the level of importance you assigned to success (Prompt 2), what one thing you feel would help you to achieve success (Prompt 3), and what advice you have for yourself (Prompt 4).

Then, complete this sentence: To be successful, I need . . .

This need could be to do, be, and/or have something. Write the first thoughts that come to mind.

To be successful, I need _____

_____

_____

_____

_____

_____

_____

_____

_____

Finding balance in success

For many people, having a successful life also means having a balanced life, in which all the different areas of life feel fulfilled and no one area is neglected. To get a better sense of your life balance and its relationship to being successful, complete these life balance activities.

Do This

One way to assess your life balance is to fill out a Life Area Success Chart, like the one in Figure 12-1. The chart is divided into seven slices, with each slice representing a life area.

Using a colored pencil or crayon, fill in each slice to the level of success you currently have in that area, where level 1 is the least amount of success and level 5 is successful.

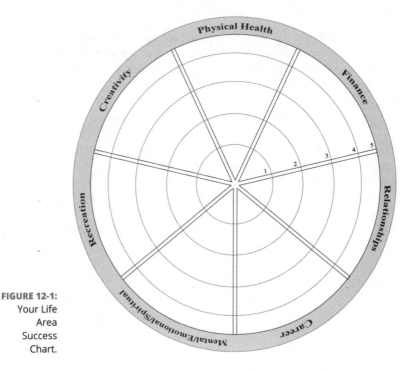

FIGURE 12-1:
Your Life
Area
Success
Chart.

Figure 12-2 provides an example of a completed chart. Notice how Physical Health and Relationships show a high level of success, while Creativity, Recreation, and Career are marked as having lower levels of success.

Refer to your completed chart and think about why you're more successful in some areas than in others. Are some areas more important to you? Do you spend considerably more time focusing on one area to the exclusion of others? With these ideas and your Life Area Success Chart in mind, respond to as many of the following prompts as you want. Take your time and work through them thoughtfully because reflecting on success and how it relates to life balance can help you decide which goals to prioritize.

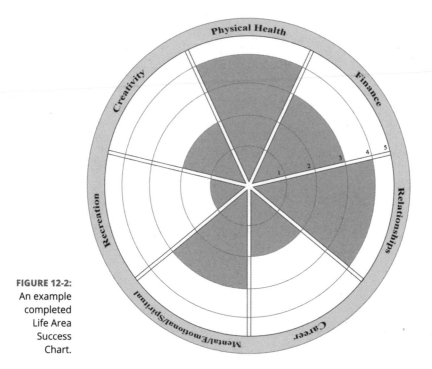

FIGURE 12-2:
An example
completed
Life Area
Success
Chart.

Prompt 1

Are you content with your overall life balance, reflected in your completed Life Area Success Chart (refer to Figure 12-1)? Why or why not, and what would you change?

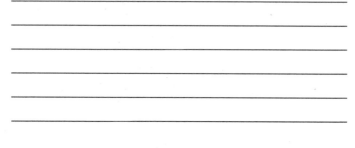

_____

_____

_____

_____

_____

_____

Prompt 2

Thinking about your success levels in each life area in your Life Area Success Chart (refer to Figure 12-1), complete the following sentences.

I am most successful in _____

_____

because_____

_____

_____

_____

I am least successful in_____

_____

because _____

_____

_____

_____

Food for thought: What do your answers reveal about your priorities and behaviors? Do you want to change any of these priorities or behaviors?

Prompt 3

For you, does being successful mean you need to be balanced, or is success correlated more strongly with one particular area of your Life Area Success Chart (refer to Figure 12-1)?

_____

If balance is important, explain how being balanced means success to you and what actions might help you achieve that balance.

_____

_____

_____

_____

_____

_____

_____

_____

If balance isn't as critical as success in one particular area, explain why success in that area is important to you. For example, if you marked Recreation as low in the Life Balance Chart, it might be because there's another area you value more and where you're placing your focus, such as a Relationship or Financial Goal.

_____

_____

_____

_____

_____

_____

Narrowing your definition of success

For the journaling activities in this section, I'm assuming that you've completed the exercises in the preceding sections in this chapter: You've defined, in general, what success looks like for you (flip back to the section "Exploring the idea of success," earlier in this chapter), and you've identified the life areas you're most and least successful in. You've also determined if those life areas are balanced, and in what ways balance is or isn't important to you (all of which I cover in the preceding section).

With those assumptions in mind, the next step is to narrow down your definition of success more precisely in each of your life areas. And then, finally, write a definition of success that captures its most meaningful and important qualities.

Do This

Define success for each area of your life.

For example, for one of my students, financial success means "being able to live a comfortable life without having to worry about money on a day-to-day basis. It means having housing and healthcare security. And it means being able to travel once or twice a year and give modest gifts to friends and family for celebrations and holidays." For you, financial success could mean something different entirely.

Complete the following sentences, starting with, For me . . .

Financial success means _____

_____

_____

_____

_____

_____

Physical health success means _____

_____

_____

_____

_____

_____

Relationship success means _____

_____

_____

_____

_____

_____

Career success means _____

_____

_____

_____

_____

_____

Mental/emotional/spiritual success means _____

_____

_____

_____

_____

_____

Recreational success means _____

_____

_____

_____

_____

_____

Creative success means _____

_____

_____

_____

_____

_____

After you define success for each life area, round up the most important elements of each definition and combine these into one concise success statement. If a life area isn't important to your sense of success, you don't need to include it in your combined success statement.

Here's an example combined statement, including all the life areas:

For me, being successful means I am financially secure and safe, able to live a comfortable yet not luxurious lifestyle; I am physically fit with no health issues and enjoy unlimited mobility; I have a solid relationship with my partner as well as a few important and supportive close relationships; I am self-employed as a part-time entrepreneur; I engage in self-care practices and am emotionally and mentally healthy; I find time to connect with nature, hike, and exercise regularly; and I make time to express myself creatively through music and crafts.

For me, being successful means _____

_____

_____

_____

_____

_____

_____

_____

_____

_____

_____

Exploring Your Core Beliefs about Success

When setting out to achieve goals and become successful, you need to consider how your past, the society and culture in which you live, and your family values have shaped both your definition of success and your core beliefs about whether you can attain them.

Core beliefs are deeply embedded, often unconscious, and at the root of our assumptions. Your core beliefs about success are tangled with other beliefs you have about your abilities, spirituality, family relationships, love, and more. All of these together comprise your *belief systems*, which drive many of your desires and behaviors.

Exploring your core belief systems through journaling is crucial for revealing your underlying mindset and uncovering unconscious internal barriers you may have to achieving your goals.

For example, do you believe you can develop and grow through meaningful effort? If so, where did that positive mindset come from?

Or do you believe that talents and abilities are part of a person's personality, something they're born with, and that if you don't have the talent for it, you won't be able to develop it? If so, what in your life experience created this fixed mindset?

Perhaps your underlying belief about yourself and your abilities to achieve success falls somewhere between these two extremes.

Whatever the case may be, it's important to be aware of your beliefs so that you can understand how they affect the way you approach success.

Identifying influential sources

To gain insight about your core beliefs, start by examining the sources that influenced you, which can help you gain understanding of why you believe what you believe and behave the ways you do — which, in turn, empowers you to consciously choose beliefs that work for you.

Do This

Respond to the following prompts to explore how your family and local culture influenced your definition of success.

Prompt 1

What messages did you get or what were you taught about success when you were growing up?

In my family success means _____

_____

_____

_____

In my culture to be successful means_____

_____

_____

_____

In my experience success is _____

_____

_____

_____

Prompt 2

Is your current definition of success aligned with your family's definition of success (the family you grew up with)? If so, why do you think you agree with them? If not, in what ways does it differ and what in your life caused you to believe differently?

_____

_____

_____

_____

_____

_____

_____

_____

_____

_____

_____

Recognizing your mindset

Do you have a positive or negative mindset about success? In other words, do you strongly believe you can be successful, or do you harbor doubts? The following prompts can help you clarify your mindset.

Do This

Complete the following four prompts to reflect on what you believe about success, your internal challenges, and your motivation to succeed.

Prompt 1

Free-write for a few minutes on what you believe about yourself in relationship to success and why.

_____

_____

_____

_____

_____

Prompt 2

Journal about any internal challenges you feel that you have in achieving your goals in the near future. For example, do you have certain habitual behaviors — such as procrastination, desire for immediate gratification, or perfectionism — that tend to slow your progress? Perhaps you tend to start out enthusiastically and then lose steam. Or maybe it's something else.

When you establish goals and create an action plan to meet those goals, being aware of your internal challenges, or barriers, will help you create a plan that realistically takes these challenges into account.

Prompt 3

Rate how motivated you are to be successful by circling the number that most closely corresponds with how willing you are to make sacrifices to achieve results.

1	2	3	4	5
Not at all willing to sacrifice	Not very willing to sacrifice	Neutral/ Don't know	Somewhat willing to sacrifice	Extremely willing to sacrifice

Free-write about why you rated your motivation the way you did and what "making sacrifices" means to you.

_____

_____

_____

_____

_____

_____

_____

_____

_____

_____

_____

_____

_____

Is there a difference between how you rated the importance of success in the section "Exploring the idea of success," earlier in this chapter, and how you rated your motivation in this prompt? If so, this disparity may reveal an inner conflict. Write about what the differences between *importance* and *motivation* mean for you and how these differences may influence your behaviors.

_____

_____

Prompt 4

Review and reflect on your responses to Prompts 1 through 3 in this section. What new awareness or insight do you have into your core beliefs, and what might you need to change in order to overcome your inner challenges?

REMEMBER

Keep in mind that core beliefs are deeply embedded beliefs and not usually easy to change — but they *can* be changed with mindful awareness and an intentional plan of action.

If you identify core beliefs that are holding you back and that you want to change, you can make this change one of your goals (you can read about goals in the following section).

Establishing Your Goals

In this section, I show you how to establish clearly defined and achievable success-related goals, and how to create action plans that can carry you to your desired ends.

The following sections contain activities that guide you through the process for one goal. If you want to establish additional goals and action plans, follow the process outlined in those sections for each goal.

WARNING

People often become enthusiastic and start setting goals without considering the amount of work it'll take to achieve those goals. Consequently, a few weeks down the line, they're exhausted and discouraged, and even give up on themselves. They've set too many goals, and they're simply overwhelmed. Don't let this happen to you.

TIP

For best results, start with a small number of goals — preferably one to three. Working toward fewer goals can help you stay focused on your top priorities and increase your chances of successfully attaining those goals.

Achievable goals answer the following:

>> What

>> When

>> How

>> Why

Defining the What

Select one life area in which you want to grow or make improvements. Then, ask yourself, "What is the *one* thing I want to accomplish in this area of my life, the one big thing that would make me feel successful in this area?" This is the *What*.

Whether the What is tangible or intangible, the answer must be specific. For example, "I want to make more money" is too vague to be actionable. What would actually constitute financial success? "I want to increase my yearly income by 10 percent" puts a definitive number on the results you're looking for.

If your goal is intangible, such as improving a behavior or changing an attitude, you need to make the intangible tangible by determining how that behavior or attitude is displayed and how it can be measured. For example, if you want to learn how to better handle your anger constructively you need to identify an observable, measurable behavior that demonstrates successful anger management. Perhaps it's communicating more effectively by speaking in a calm voice instead of yelling, which can be measured by keeping a record of times when you feel angry and how you behave. In this case, you might write: "When I feel angry, I want to communicate in a calm voice instead of yelling, at least 90 percent of the time." (You've defined success as changing your behavior a majority of the time, rather than expecting perfection.)

Do This

Now, for the life area you selected, write down your What — the one thing that you want to have or accomplish that would make you feel successful. This is your goal.

What: _____

_____

_____

Deciding on When

The next task is determining the *When* — the due-by date.

Without a due date, a What isn't a goal, it's only a wish. Your due date functions to motivate you to stay on track and hold yourself accountable. For your What, ask yourself in what realistic time-frame you can achieve it. Some goals can be accomplished in a few weeks; others take a year or more. The key to success with deciding your When is to be as realistic as possible.

Here's what adding the When (due date) to the What (goal) looks like: "I want to increase my yearly income by 10 percent by the end of next year."

TIP

Due dates aren't set in stone. They're simply targets to aim for. If, after starting on a goal, you realize that you set an unrealistic date or circumstances set you back, you can change that date to a more doable, realistic time.

However, if you find yourself constantly shifting due dates, use your journal to reflect on what's holding you back from completing your goal-related tasks on time. (Flip to Chapter 5 for an in-depth discussion of reflective journaling and prompt ideas.)

Do This

Write down by when you plan to achieve your goal.

I will achieve my goal by _____

Figuring out the How

Goals (the Whats, which you can read about in the section "Defining the What," earlier in this chapter) are big-picture items, such as making a certain amount of money, achieving a certain position in a career, having a certain possession, or attaining a particular skill. A goal is like a destination — like saying, "I want to go to New York." To get to any destination, you need to know the method of transportation you have to take to get there.

Your *How* is your method — the actions you will take toward achieving your What.

Here's the example from the preceding section, now including the How: "I want to increase my income by 10 percent by one year from today. I will accomplish this by gaining the necessary skills and applying for a management position in my company."

Do This

What's the How for your goal? Write it here.

I will accomplish my goal by _____

_____

_____

_____

_____

Understanding the Why

Goals take work to achieve. They're not easy. There will be times when you lose heart, times when you wonder why you're going through so much effort, and times you'll feel discouraged or set back. During those times, you need to turn to your reason for setting that goal in the first place.

Your *Why* — your reason for chasing that achievement — is what drives and propels you forward. When you're very clear about why you want what you want, you have more energy to continue working toward it. On the other hand, if you aren't clear, if your reasons for wanting something are vague or aren't internalized, you may not have a strong enough desire to do what it takes to get to your destination.

Do This

Clarify your Why by completing the following sentence.

My What is important to me because _____

_____

_____

_____

_____

_____

All together now! Writing your goal statement

Now, put the What, When, How, and Why from the preceding sections together into one complete goal statement.

Here's an example of what that statement looks like:

I want to learn conversational Spanish and be able to hold simple conversations by the end of this year. I will accomplish this by taking language classes at the community college and joining an online English–Spanish conversation group. This is important to me because the job I want requires the ability to understand and speak Spanish.

_____

_____

_____

_____

_____

_____

Creating Your Plan of Action

A *plan of action* is simply a list of sequential tasks needed to get something done or, in this case, to achieve a goal.

When you have a statement that clearly defines your goal, including the What, When, How, and Why (discussed in the section "Establishing Your Goals," earlier in this chapter), then you're ready to add this information to your journal and create your plan of action.

If your goal is to learn conversational Spanish, for example, your plan of action might look like this:

» Go online and look at the local community college's class schedule.

» Apply for enrollment at the community college.

>> Apply for the specific Spanish-language class that I want to take.

>> Research possible online and local English–Spanish conversation groups and decide which one works best for me.

>> Apply to join the group.

>> Schedule daily language practice (maybe find a practice buddy?).

Notice that all of these actions are simple, and each one can be done in a relatively short period of time. Along the way, you can add more action items or break a larger task into subtasks, as needed.

Do This

Create a Goals section in your journal. Alternatively, you can keep a dedicated journal just for your goals. (If you're using the Bullet Journal method discussed in Chapter 7, create a new collection for your goal and enter the page number in your BuJo index.) Write the appropriate life area from your Life Area Success Chart (refer to Figure 12-1) as a title at the top of a blank page, and then copy your goal statement from the preceding section below the title.

Beneath your goal statement, brainstorm a list of specific actions that you need to take to achieve your goal. Remember to keep the actions simple and short.

Get Moving! Putting Your Action Plan into Action

When you've written your plan of action, the next step is to simply begin doing the planned actions, one task at a time.

TIP

Here are a few tips to help you get started and stay on track:

>> Identify the *quick-win tasks* (the tasks that are easy and/or quick to complete) and do these first.

>> Complete each task before moving to the next one.

>> If you encounter a barrier to completing a task (say, having to wait for a response from someone), then mark the task for later review and move your focus to the next task.

>> If an action is too complex to be accomplished in 20 minutes or less, break it down into subtasks.

The following sections help you track and measure your success, as well as make necessary adjustments along the way.

Holding yourself accountable

The word *accountability* can feel intimidating to a lot of people, so I want to alleviate any concerns you have about it right away.

Accountability simply means that you take ownership and responsibility for the results of your actions. In other words, you don't expect your goals to just happen all by themselves. You know that you need to apply yourself to the tasks in a timely way in order to achieve your goal within your timeline, and you do so.

When you hold yourself accountable for accomplishing each task on your action plan, you increase your self-motivation and confidence. Being accountable helps you measure progress along the way. And when you've been accountable and successfully completed one goal, the next goal becomes easier because you know how to do it.

Reviewing your progress

As the saying goes, "Out of sight, out of mind." The key to making progress on a goal, whether short- or long-term, is to keep that goal visible. Keep it in sight and in your mind.

Keeping your goals and action plans in your journal is a good start. Create an ongoing to-do list and transfer tasks from your action plan to your list — or use your daily log in your Bullet Journal (Flip to Chapter 7 for details on how to set up and use daily logs.)

While you check off items on your to-do list, also cross them off your action plan. Checking off items makes it easy to see your progress.

TIP

The Bullet Journal method lends itself extremely well to tracking projects and goals. Read Chapter 7 to get the lowdown on this method.

REMEMBER

Set aside time to review your goal(s) and tasks regularly — weekly, at a minimum. Daily is even better. Keep your eye on your What and review your Why regularly, as well. Reminding yourself constantly of your reasons for wanting your goal can help you maintain momentum.

Celebrating your success

Along the way, reward yourself for small accomplishments. Did you push through on a task that you didn't really want to do? Give yourself a small indulgence, such as making time to watch your favorite TV series or taking a walk in the park. Are you halfway to your goal? Time to reward yourself! Go out for dinner, enjoy a movie, give yourself an at-home spa day (or, if you can afford it, go to an actual spa).

When you reward yourself, dopamine floods your brain, which causes a surge in pleasure. This, in turn, provides a sense of satisfaction, gives you more motivation, and enhances your productivity.

And when you finally accomplish your What, be sure to pause and take time to celebrate your success. Reward yourself with an extravagance of some kind that corresponds with the importance of your goal.

Chapter **13**

Exploring Spirituality

What is spirit? According to the Oxford English online dictionary, *spirit* is "the nonphysical part of a person regarded as their true self and as capable of surviving physical death or separation." A secondary meaning is "those qualities regarded as forming the definitive or typical elements in the character of a person."

Both definitions refer to the inner part of a person that can't be seen and is integral to who they are and how they interact with and appear to others in the world.

Although the idea of spirituality is often aligned with religion (in fact, according to the Pew Research Center, 84 percent of people around the world belong to one of the many organized religions), for many people, being spiritual doesn't necessarily mean also being religious — or even believing in a god or spirit or soul. For example, some humanists and atheists identify mindfulness practice or humanitarian acts as spiritual in nature. So, how spirituality is defined is deeply personal for each individual.

Whether you identify with a particular religion or not, journaling about spirituality and what it means to you can bring fresh perspective to your life, help identify areas of personal growth, and facilitate defining your life purpose.

In this chapter, you have the opportunity to use journaling prompts to articulate your own definition of spirituality, as well as what it means to connect spiritually, reflect on ways to accelerate your spiritual growth, and discover (or rediscover) your life mission and purpose.

TIP

In preparation for journaling about spiritual topics, before each writing session, take a few minutes to center and bring yourself present. Use mindful journaling techniques (see Chapter 6 for details on this method) and/or create a ritual, as described in Chapter 4, to connect with your spirituality. You may choose to focus on a candle flame, meditate briefly, pray, or engage in another short mindfulness practice — whatever works for you. You just need to tap into the spiritual part of your being before beginning to journal.

If you prefer to explore spirituality using creative journaling, draw or create other visual representations of your answers in your personal creative journal (turn to Chapter 8 for an in-depth overview of this method).

Defining What Spirituality Means for You

Like any abstract concept, the word spirituality means different things to different people. If you were raised in a particular religion, your definition of spirituality probably sprang from that upbringing, and those around you believed the same thing. As a result, you probably grew up making unconscious assumptions that everyone else has the same interpretation of spirituality that you do.

But different religions have different interpretations. And even humanists, who don't believe in a non-material or unseen world, grapple with how to define spirituality.

So to begin your journaling exploration, articulate your personal understanding of spirituality and how it affects and is expressed in your life.

Do This

The following journaling prompts help you think about and verbalize what spirituality means for you personally. Respond to Prompts 1 through 7 in any order you choose. In Prompt 8 you have an opportunity to write your definition as a statement.

Prompt 1

Describe how you imagine *spirit* or *soul* would look like, if you could see it, and where it's located in the body. Feel free to write your answer or represent it with a drawing.

Prompt 2

What images do you associate with the word *spirituality*? For example, do you picture ethereal beings, stained glass windows, a person meditating, or someone providing food to the homeless?

_____

_____

_____

_____

_____

_____

Prompt 3

Consider the ways your parents' and close relatives' beliefs influenced your spiritual attitudes and beliefs as you grew up. As an adult, do you reject or embrace those beliefs, and why?

_____

_____

_____

_____

_____

_____

_____

_____

Prompt 4

Do you believe in an afterworld, or life after death? Why or why not?

_____

_____

_____

_____

_____

_____

Prompt 5

Write an argument for both sides of the following question: Do you think it's important to act on spiritual beliefs?

Yes, because_____

_____

_____

_____

No, because _____

_____

_____

_____

Prompt 6

What does it mean to be a spiritual person?

_____

_____

_____

_____

_____

_____

Prompt 7

Do you think that being spiritual and having life purpose are related? Explain your answer.

_____

_____

_____

_____

_____

_____

Prompt 8

Review and reflect on your responses to Prompts 1 through 7 in this section, then define what spirituality means to you by completing the following sentence:

Spirituality is _____

_____

_____

_____

TIP

Copy your definition of spirituality into your personal journal for future reference. If you wish, create a special section dedicated to exploring your spirituality.

Focusing on Spiritual Connection

Have you ever felt deeply connected to another person? Or deeply connected with a being or energy greater than yourself? These connections — which can be with a person, place, or thing — are called *spiritual connections* because they resonate profoundly within us.

In this section, you use journaling prompts to explore and describe what connection means for you and what mechanisms or actions you take to deepen your spiritual connections. Through journaling, you can heighten your connection-awareness, which will help you recognize meaningful spiritual connections as they happen.

Do This

Each of the following prompts is designed to help raise self-awareness about your experiences with being spiritually connected. Complete any of the prompts that resonate for you (they each explore connection from a different angle).

REMEMBER

Center yourself in the moment before responding to the prompts because centering can help you tap into deeper, intuitive insights. (See Chapter 6 for ways to focus on the present.)

Prompt 1

How do you know when you're connected spiritually, either with yourself, someone else, or a higher power? Describe what spiritual connection feels like to you.

_____

_____

_____

_____

_____

_____

_____

Prompt 2

Describe any specific rituals or actions that help you feel connected with spirit. For example, perhaps you read from a religious text, light a candle, or meditate. What about your rituals/actions attracts you?

_____

_____

_____

_____

_____

_____

Prompt 3

List five to ten people, places, or things that you've always connected to on a deep level. What draws you to them, and in what
ways do you maintain and deepen those connections?

_____

_____

_____

_____

_____

_____

_____

_____

_____

Prompt 4

Write about a moment or time in your life in which you felt spiritually connected to one of the people, places, or things you
listed in response to Prompt 3. What was happening, where were
you, who or what were you connected to, and how did that
moment affect you?

_____

_____

_____

_____

_____

_____

_____

_____

Journaling for Spiritual Growth

Reflective journaling (discussed in Chapter 5) can be an effective tool for spiritual growth, which means developing and strengthening those aspects of your spirituality that you feel are important. Writing reflectively helps clarify the thoughts and feelings that you have about your spiritual life and beliefs. It also allows you to track changes and growth in your spiritual insights by documenting them along the way, and help you to stay focused on any spiritual goals you may have.

In the following sections, I provide journaling prompts in two areas of growth: building on and enhancing your strengths, and understanding and embracing your shadow side. I explain the importance of both these areas — and why to address them — in their respective sections.

Building on your strengths

One of the best ways to grow spiritually is to identify your strengths and then enhance those strengths. Typically, the characteristics or areas in which you're strong are also a big part of how you identify yourself. You feel pleasure in your strengths, and enhancing them through practice can empower you to fulfill your life purpose. Journaling can help you with this process — from identifying your strengths to figuring out which ones you want to build and deciding on actions you want to take that will help you grow.

The following journaling prompts focus on your strengths and how you might use them to become a stronger person, spiritually.

Do This

Respond to each of the following prompts in order, as each prompt builds upon the previous one.

Prompt 1

Review the following list of qualities that are commonly considered spiritual, and then:

> >> Add any qualities that you think are missing from the list.

> >> Circle all the qualities that you're already strong in.

> >> Underline the ones that you want to develop.

Spiritual qualities

Authentic	Loving
Caring	Non-judgmental
Compassionate	Open
Empathetic	Optimistic
Generous	Patient
Grateful	Peaceful
Humble	Present
Just	Respectful
Kind	Unselfish

_____

_____

_____

Prompt 2

Consider the qualities that you circled in Prompt 1. Which of these qualities are you strongest in? In what ways could you express that strength more in your life?

_____

_____

_____

_____

_____

_____

_____

_____

_____

_____

_____

_____

Prompt 3

What changes would you need to make in your life to develop the qualities that you underlined in Prompt 1? For example, what attitudes or activities would you need to give up, and what would you need to do more of?

_____

_____

_____

_____

_____

_____

_____

_____

_____

_____

_____

_____

Embracing your shadow

Every person has a shadow side. It's the part of you that contains qualities or characteristics that are unconscious, or that you don't like or feel ashamed about and want to hide from the world (including from yourself). You might think about it as your inner darkness, lower self, repressed self, or id. And though you may find it natural to judge this shadow side of yourself as negative, every seemingly negative characteristic has a positive side, and every part of you is essential to who you are as a whole.

Bringing what's hidden in the shadows into the light of consciousness is important to help you grow both spiritually and emotionally. And all the things you don't like about yourself, when uncovered and consciously acknowledged, can be expressed positively instead of negatively. Recognizing and embracing your shadow side, and integrating those qualities into your awareness, contributes to healing and wholeness.

Journaling can help you accomplish this work by giving you a safe space in which to explore and examine these aspects of your character. For example, all my life I had judged myself as bossy and loud, and I had suppressed these "negative" parts of my personality. But when I metaphorically pulled them out of the shadows and examined them more closely in my journaling practice, I realized that they were actually uncontrolled representations of assertiveness and passion — both leadership qualities. Embracing these traits and learning how to manage them contributed to my later success as a department manager.

Do This

The following prompts provide an introduction to exploring your shadow side and discovering what it has to offer. I suggest doing all three prompts in order, because each one helps you to consider your shadow side from a different perspective.

Prompt 1

Do you struggle with anger, jealousy, or other emotions that you consider negative? What parts of yourself do you not want to see or admit you have?

_____

_____

_____

_____

_____

_____

Prompt 2

Most often, when characteristics and behaviors of other people upset or annoy you, it's because you also have these traits, but you've stashed them in your shadow side. Write about some of the things other people do (or are) that you have a strong negative reaction to. Then, journal about the ways you are like them.

_____

_____

_____

_____

_____

_____

_____

_____

_____

Prompt 3

Select one of the negative characteristics you identified in either of the previous prompts and that you suspect may also be a part of you. List the positive ways that characteristic can be acknowledged and expressed. For example, if you identified "controlling" as a negative trait, think about some of the beneficial ways control can be expressed: being organized, action-oriented, and reliable come to mind.

TIP

If you're having a difficult time coming with up with positive ways to express a characteristic, perform an Internet search for *benefits of [name of characteristic]* to stimulate ideas.

Repeat this prompt using additional characteristics you've identified as part of your shadow side.

_____

_____

_____

_____

_____

_____

_____

_____

Journal about how you can begin to apply positive expressions of the characteristic you identified previously.

_____

_____

_____

_____

_____

_____

Developing Spiritual Mission and Purpose Statements

Businesses develop mission and purpose statements to define their business focus and provide company executives with a decision-making road map that aligns with the company's values.

Similarly, spiritual mission and purpose statements are like having a road map for making life decisions that align with your spiritual focus and values. Together, they give you a document that you can refer to any time you need to make a significant decision — or just to ensure that you're staying true to your spiritual self.

So, what are spiritual mission and purpose statements?

>> Your *mission* statement defines your spiritual focus by describing the impact you want to make in the world, who you want to impact, and how that impact will help them.

>> Your *purpose* statement describes the kind of person you want to be and how you want to live your life in order to achieve your mission.

Both statements should be big-picture and broad enough to allow flexibility, but specific enough to provide guidance later on.

Journaling is a helpful way to figure out your mission and purpose, and then to write them out in statement form. When created thoughtfully and with intention, your mission and purpose statements can remain relevant for many years, guiding you through life challenges and critical decision points.

In the following sections, I walk you through a four-step journaling process to develop your spiritual mission and purpose statements.

TIP

If possible, complete the following prompts and process in one long, reflective session. This session can take from two to four hours. However, you can also accomplish these steps in two or three shorter sessions; whatever fits your schedule.

Step 1: Explore what drives you

Having a sense of purpose is integral to humans' sense of spirituality. Yet, sometimes we struggle with understanding what our personal purpose might be. In this changing and confusing world, we may wonder, "How can I help?" or "What difference can I make?"

Journaling can help you gain perspective on who you are and what you care about most deeply. And it's in the things you care most deeply about that your purpose lies.

By using the following prompts, you can outline your values and strengths, what brings you joy and satisfaction, your relationship priorities, and ways that you can make a difference. Use this information, along with insights gained from your responses to "Step 2: Look back on a life well lived" to create your mission and purpose statements in the sections "Step 3: Create your spiritual mission statement" and "Step 4: Write your spiritual purpose statement" later in this chapter.

Do This

Complete the following sentences. Don't overthink when responding to the prompts. Trust your intuition, include what matters to you spiritually, and simply write down the first things that come to mind.

The values that are most important to me in life are _____

_____

_____

_____

My greatest strengths, including skills and competencies are

_____

_____

_____

_____

The things that bring me the most joy and satisfaction are _____

_____

_____

_____

_____

_____

I want my relationships with others to be _____

_____

_____

_____

Ways I could make a difference in the world include _____

_____

_____

_____

_____

_____

Step 2: Look back on a life well lived

One way to discover what's most important to you is to think about what a spiritually fulfilled life might look like. This activity prompts you to reflect on what you want to achieve in life and what kind of person you want to be from a spiritual perspective.

To get started, imagine that you're coming to the end of a long, full, and satisfying life in which you accomplished your dreams and contributed to the world in a meaningful way. You feel at peace spiritually and are happy with how you lived your life and what you achieved.

Take time here to close your eyes and fully imagine this future self. Feel the peace and sense of satisfaction of having lived this full life. Consider the impact you made on the earth and/or people around you and how you went about effecting that impact.

Do This

From the perspective of your imagined future self, write a summary of your "life well lived" as though you're looking back. Take your time with this prompt. What kind of life did you live? Include your achievements, obstacles you overcame, your closest relationships, what you did for fun, and how you made your mark on the world (what legacy you left).

_____

_____

_____

_____

_____

_____

_____

_____

_____

_____

_____

_____

_____

_____

_____

_____

_____

_____

_____

_____

_____

_____

_____

_____

_____

_____

_____

_____

_____

Review what you wrote in your summary and highlight (or circle) words and phrases that mirror the values, strengths, joys, relationships, and contributions to others that you wrote in the preceding section. Refer back to these common words and phrases when you write your mission and purpose statements in the following activities in Step 3 and Step 4.

Step 3: Create your spiritual mission statement

Using the information from the section "Step 1: Explore what drives you," earlier in this chapter, and Step 2 in the preceding section, begin to create your spiritual mission statement. Focus especially on the highlighted words and phrases from the life summary that you wrote in in the preceding section. I recommend using the following format (see Figure 13-1 for an example):

"My mission is to [*impact*] [*who*] to [*what*] by [*how*]."

Here's how the elements of this statement break down:

>> **Impact:** The effect that your actions have on others. Impact words include *help, influence, facilitate,* and *empower.* You can use one of these words or choose a word that better fits the impact of your mission.

>> **Who:** The people or subset of people whom your actions affect. The example mission statement in Figure 13-1 uses "people." Your mission might be specific to women, students, children, or some other subset of a population.

>> **What:** The things that your Who can do as a result of your impact on them.

>> **How:** The ways in which you impact your Who to accomplish the What.

FIGURE 13-1:
A mission statement example, showing the different parts of the statement format.

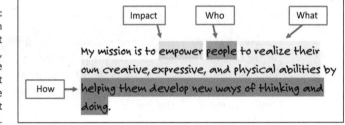

Do This

Write your mission statement in the space provided by using the [*impact*], [*who*], [*what*], and [*how*] format.

My mission is to_____

_____

_____

_____

_____

_____

_____

Review your mission statement. How does it feel to you? Mission statements, by their nature, are lofty, something you aspire to.

When in alignment with your core spiritual values, strengths, and life dreams, your statement should feel true and authentic to who you are and who you want to be. It should feel like a good fit.

If it doesn't feel like a good fit, it might mean that you've missed including an important value or you haven't quite captured how you might accomplish your mission. Review Steps 1 and 2 in the preceding sections, and then rewrite or revise your statement until it does fit.

Step 4: Write your spiritual purpose statement

Your spiritual purpose statement should build on and expand from your spiritual mission statement (see the preceding section) and answer the question, "How do I need to live my life in order to fulfill my mission?" The following prompt helps you explore this question.

Do This

What do I need to understand and do in order to be the kind of person I imagine I can become in Step 2? (Flip back to the section "Step 2: Look back on a life well lived," earlier in this chapter, for more on your imagined future self.) Free-write your response in the space provided.

_____

_____

_____

_____

_____

_____

_____

_____

Reflecting on what you wrote in response to this prompt and your mission statement (see the preceding section), write your purpose statement by using the following format:

"The purpose of my life is to [*what*] by [*mission*]."

Your purpose statement needs to include these elements:

>> **What:** What you need to do and/or how you need to live in order to accomplish your mission. You may include more than one What in your purpose statement.

>> **Mission:** Circles back to the outcome or result of your mission statement.

Figure 13-2 provides an example of a purpose statement written using this format. Note that there are two What phrases. Include as many What phrases as is appropriate to you. The phrase "helping others grow in their creative and physical abilities" is taken from the last line of the mission statement in Figure 13-1. It's okay to paraphrase or summarize your mission results here.

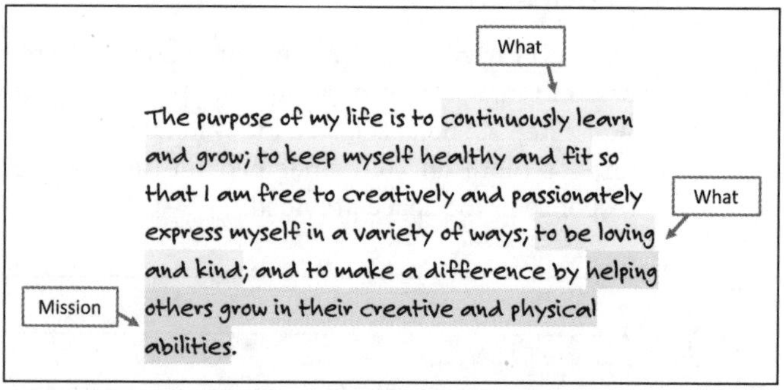

FIGURE 13-2:
A purpose statement using the [*what*] by [*mission*] format.

What

The purpose of my life is to continuously learn and grow; to keep myself healthy and fit so that I am free to creatively and passionately express myself in a variety of ways; to be loving and kind; and to make a difference by helping others grow in their creative and physical abilities.

What

Mission

Write your purpose statement using the [*what*] by [*mission*] format.

The purpose of my life is to _____

_____

_____

_____

_____

_____

_____

_____

Creating a Spiritual Journal

A spiritual journal is simply a place where you record your personal thoughts and reactions to spiritual matters. It's where you connect in writing with your spiritual practice, whether that's sharing your thoughts and prayers to a god, writing meditations, or tapping into and writing from a place of inner wisdom.

Your spiritual journal is a place to write about

>> Responses to things you read in religious texts

>> Observations of things around you from a spiritual perspective

>> Spiritual insights gained from life events

>> Prayers

>> Spiritual poems and essays

>> Insights discovered while looking back at previous journal entries (in any type of journal)

>> Reactions to religion and religious events

>> Spiritual connections

>> Anything related to your spiritual mission and purpose (see the previous section, "Developing Spiritual Mission and Purpose Statements")

>> Spiritual dreams

Keep in mind that a spiritual journal is different from a daily journal (whatever journal you use on a regular basis), which acts as more a record of events, thoughts, and feelings about life. A spiritual journal, on the other hand, is dedicated solely to matters you consider spiritual in nature.

TIP

If you don't want to keep a lot of separate notebooks, you can create a spiritual journal section inside your daily journal. And if you keep a Bullet Journal, create a Spiritual Thoughts collection and record the page numbers in your index. (Flip to Chapter 7 for how to create and use the Bullet Journaling method.)

Start your journal by writing your definition of spirituality (which I go over in the section "Defining What Spirituality Means for You," earlier in this chapter). If you did the exercises in the section "Developing Spiritual Mission and Purpose Statements," earlier in this chapter, also add your mission and purpose statements to the first page so that you can refer back to these often.

Chapter **14**

Navigating Grief

G rief is a special kind of sorrow that arises from loss — an anguish that can seem like a black, bottomless hole ready to swallow you up.

This chapter offers journaling prompts for recognizing and affirming your grief, techniques for self-care and how to be compassionate with yourself, and creative prompts to help you understand and find meaning in your grief. Because when you can find meaning in your loss, you can also find a path to healing.

Identifying Your Loss

Grief is most often associated with loss of a loved one, but there are many kinds of loss that cause grief. In addition to death, grief-inducing losses may include:

» Divorce

» Job or income loss

>> A relationship breakup

>> Death of a life dream

>> Ill health or loss of mobility due to accident or illness

>> Loss of a home

>> Aging (loss of youth and vitality)

>> Birth of a child who has severe illness or disability

The list of ways to experience loss is endless, and there are just as many ways to feel and express grief.

If a loss is great enough, you might not feel its full effects for days or weeks due to being in shock or having to focus on simply getting through each day. And if you experience more than one loss at one time, that delayed-feeling effect is increased. On the other hand, maybe you can't focus at work, you can't stop crying, or you go through your days in a dull fog. You might experience physical symptoms, such as unusual fatigue, chest pain, and headaches.

All of these emotions and physical reactions are completely natural and normal responses to grief. Everyone experiences grief in their own unique way, and no one's grief is more or less valid than anyone else's, regardless of the reason for it.

REMEMBER

Journaling your thoughts and feelings can help you navigate through the tough emotions that come with grief. Your journal is the one completely private and safe place where you can give voice to your deepest feelings without the burden of others' judgment or kindest intentions. In your journal, you can express all of it: rage, confusion, denial, sadness, depression, guilt, along with the unexpected ray of joy that occasionally pierces the darkness.

Acknowledging and Validating Your Feelings

Denial, one of the recognized phases of grief, can take the form of refusing to believe a loss has occurred, but it can also mean denying the feelings that come with grief.

For example, a person might be dealing with handling an estate and making all the arrangements after the death of a loved one, and they have others depending on them to be strong, so they think they don't have the time to give into their feelings.

Another might be grieving over a loss that they think they shouldn't be this upset over. Perhaps they're having to give up on a dream, lost a job, or failed at an important endeavor. "This isn't like losing a loved one," they tell themselves, and thus they minimize the loss, deny their grief, and attempt to stuff their feelings into a metaphorical box and bury them.

Whatever the reason, denying your grief doesn't work. Your feelings refuse to be buried for long and manifest themselves in other ways in your life, only delaying your healing process. So the first step in understanding how to manage loss is to acknowledge that you're grieving and give yourself the compassion and the emotional space to experience all the feelings that you need to experience.

After you acknowledge and validate your feelings, you can begin to avail yourself of tools for healing. You can become a stronger, more empathetic, and more compassionate person in the end. And although no one who has been through grief will tell you that it goes away, it does tend to soften over time.

The following reflective journaling prompts help you acknowledge and affirm your feelings. (Turn to Chapter 5 for a look at how to journal reflectively.)

Do This

Respond to both of the following prompts in the order they're presented.

Prompt 1

Set a timer for 10 minutes and write the story of your loss. Who or what did you lose, how did it happen, and why did this person or thing (dream, opportunity, object, and so on) mean so much to you?

_____

_____

_____

_____

Review and reflect on your story. What stands out for you about it? For example, perhaps there are characteristics of the person or thing that you hadn't thought of before, or you have a deeper understanding of why you're feeling the loss so deeply. Perhaps you notice something else. Write about your reflections in the space provided.

_____

_____

_____

_____

_____

_____

_____

_____

Prompt 2

Acknowledge and affirm the emotions you've experienced as a result of your loss by writing a sentence for each feeling that names and validates that feeling.

Example: _My feelings of sadness are valid and I have every right to these feelings._

TIP

Write out the whole sentence for each emotion. The act of writing the words helps to confirm your emotions' validity.

_____

_____

_____

_____

_____

_____

_____

_____

_____

_____

_____

_____

Take time to reflect. What are you feeling in this moment after acknowledging each of your emotions? Do you feel assured or comforted, for example, and how does your experience with validating your feelings affect your overall attitude toward grieving? Add your response here.

_____

_____

_____

_____

_____

_____

Allowing Self-Compassion

It's one thing to acknowledge your feelings; it's another to be compassionate with yourself.

First, it's important to understand that you can't control the depth of your grief, and you can't control how long it will last. Therefore, there's no use in placing expectations on yourself about how you should be feeling, when you should be healed, or anything else.

REMEMBER

Any time you catch yourself thinking you should feel or be something different than you are, be aware that you're judging yourself. And when you're judging, you're not being compassionate. The key to giving yourself compassion is to see and treat yourself as you would someone else who's going through what you are.

Do This

Use the following prompt to help you see yourself more kindly and increase your self-compassion.

Imagine that you have a dear friend who's experiencing a loss like yours. Write a letter to this friend, expressing your thoughts and giving them advice about how to take care of and treat themselves while grieving. Include how you would like to help them.

_____

_____

_____

_____

_____

_____

_____

_____

_____

_____

_____

_____

_____

_____

_____

_____

_____

_____

_____

_____

_____

_____

_____

Looking back on what you wrote, what insights did you gain from writing a compassionate letter to your friend? In what ways can you release judgment and treat yourself more compassionately? Will you help yourself the same way that you offered to help your friend? Record your responses in the space provided.

_____

_____

_____

_____

_____

_____

_____

_____

Having a Conversation with Grief

In this section, you engage in a creative journaling method that can help you gain a new perspective on your grief. Instead of thinking about grief as something you must "get over" or "get through," an obstacle to being "normal" or living the life you used to have, you can use this method to find meaning in your grief.

This approach to gaining a deeper understanding of your feelings makes use of something called _personification_ — where you give human characteristics to something that's not human, such as objects, animals, or abstract concepts.

Personification works because it allows you to see your emotion objectively. In my experience, personifying your grief and having a conversation with it has the potential to transform your relationship with it from one of opposition to one of cooperation.

The idea is this: What if Grief was a person with whom you have a relationship? Although this person can be very difficult to live with, they also have some positive qualities to share — if you can be open to them. What might happen if you got to know Grief better so that you can understand why they are who they are?

Do This

The following journaling prompts guide you through a gentle conversation with Grief. I recommend doing the prompts in order. You may need more than one journaling session to complete all the prompts.

Prompt 1

Begin by closing your eyes and imagining that Grief is a being. When you're ready, describe the being you imagine in detail. Is it male, female, other, or genderless? Describe its physical appearance — large, small, dark, light, solid, or transparent. What are its features, and what clothing does it wear? Doing this gives human-like form to a formless concept. Your Grief's form is a unique expression of how you see the effects of your loss, and gives you a way to interact with it.

_____

_____

_____

_____

_____

_____

_____

_____

Prompt 2

Give your Grief persona a name. It can be the first name that pops into your head or maybe Grief gives you a name. A step beyond providing a visual form for Grief (by responding to the previous prompt), giving your Grief a name makes it more familiar to you. A name allows you to address it directly, which you have the opportunity to do in upcoming Prompt 4.

_____

_____

Prompt 3

Imagine you have invited Grief to come over later in the day for a conversation. Make a list of questions that you want to ask. Articulating questions you have about your Grief can help you define the feelings and issues you're grappling with and want to gain understanding about.

Here are a few suggested questions (add other questions that occur to you):

>> Why did you come into my life?

>> What do you want me to know?

>> In what ways can you help me deal with my loss?

>> How do you want me to relate to you?

_____

_____

_____

_____

_____

_____

Prompt 4

Imagine Grief has arrived for a conversation. You're sitting across from each other. Your Grief says, "I'm completely open. What would you like to know?"

Ask your questions (you can use the list from Prompt 3) and write down how you imagine Grief would reply.

_____

_____

_____

_____

_____

_____

_____

_____

_____

_____

_____

_____

_____

_____

_____

_____

In writing, now tell Grief how you feel when it's near. Perhaps you feel afraid or nervous or sad. Next, explain what kind of relationship you want to have with your Grief, and ask if it's willing to help you move forward in your life. Grief typically wants to help, but if your Grief says no, continue your conversation, asking questions to figure out what Grief needs in order to help you move forward.

Continue your dialogue with your Grief as long as you feel you want or need to.

_____

_____

Through this journaling process of establishing a cooperative relationship with Grief, you can perhaps come to an acceptance of Grief and its associated feelings, understand its purpose, and even appreciate how it can help you heal. And, working with Grief instead of resisting it can help you have more patience with the healing process.

When you finish your conversation with Grief, thank them and say goodbye. Spend a few minutes in quiet contemplation, allowing your conversation experience to sink in, before responding to the next prompt.

Prompt 5

Review and reflect on your responses to Prompts 1 through 4. What did you find out about grieving and/or yourself from your conversation with Grief? Perhaps you discovered that Grief could help you adjust to your loss or that you don't have to feel afraid of your feelings. Add your thoughts in the space provided.

_____

_____

_____

_____

_____

_____

_____

_____

_____

_____

_____

_____

Expressing Grief Safely

When you feel grief's painful emotions, especially intense ones such as confusion, rage, and anxiety, it can be difficult to know what to do with all that emotional energy. If not expressed in healthy ways, it can burst out in harmful or socially inappropriate ways, such as lashing out at someone you love or breaking something. Or you might isolate, exacerbating feelings of loneliness and abandonment.

You may not be able to control the feelings resulting from your grief, but you *can* control how you respond to them and what you do with them, and that's where figuring out how to express your grief safely through journaling comes in.

The prompts in the following sections are designed to help you process and express your feelings in healthy ways.

Try a sentence-starter prompt

It can be difficult to begin writing about feelings associated with grief, because they can seem all jumbled together. Sentence-starter prompts can help you focus in on a specific feeling by providing context (a time of day, a situation, and so on) for when that feeling might be strongest.

As the name suggests, *sentence-starter prompts* begin a sentence that you then finish, and may include fill-in-the-blank sections.

Do This

Set a timer for 10 minutes, select one of the following sentence-starter prompts, and free-write without stopping for the full 10 minutes, allowing the writing to take you where it will.

>> Whenever I feel _____ I want to . . .

>> The worst time of day is _____ because . . .

>> When I'm feeling most anxious, I can calm and nurture myself by . . .

>> I feel rage whenever . . .

>> I wish people would just . . .

>> If my grief was an animal, it would be a _____, and it would . . .

>> The best way to describe how I'm feeling right now is . . .

_____

_____

_____

Review and reflect on your answer. How do you feel about expressing your grief in the safe space of your journal? Perhaps you gained a few insights from writing about your feelings and/ or the situations in which they occur. (Insights are simply new ways of perceiving or understanding something.)

Write your reflections about this journaling activity in the space provided:

_____

_____

_____

_____

_____

_____

Color your feelings

Sometimes, words just aren't enough to communicate feelings. Fortunately, journaling isn't always about words. Instead, you can use color and shapes to express yourself visually. Creative journaling (covered in Chapter 8) uses crayons, colored pencils, or paints to help you express the otherwise inexpressible and process your most complex emotions — privately and safely, in your journal.

Do This

In the space provided, use color and lines to communicate how you're feeling about your loss. You don't need to have art or drawing skills to do this activity effectively. You can create images or abstract shapes, overlay and blend colors. Or you can make a collage from pictures cut from magazines or printed off the Internet. Add speech bubbles and text, or color over them. Allow yourself to be creative.

TIP

As an added bonus, if you're working with a psychologist or therapist, sharing your visual journal entry can assist the process of understanding and healing that's taking place.

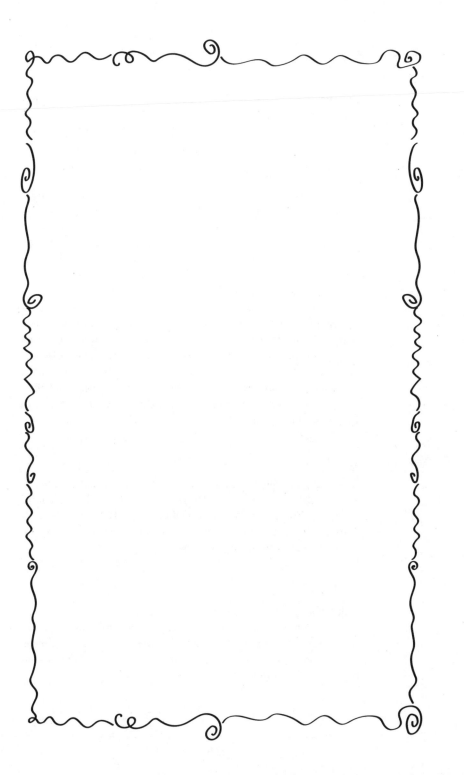

Dealing with Numbness

Another emotion — or rather, lack of emotion — that accompanies grief is numbness. It can happen at any time during the grief process, but it often occurs near the beginning after the initial shock of loss has worn off, leaving you feeling dry and empty as a desert.

Numbness is the inability to feel. If this is happening, you might be wondering if there's something wrong with you. Rest assured that feeling nothing is a normal defense mechanism, a way of shutting down emotions when they're overwhelming. In a way, numbness is an emotional anesthetic, offering relief from the raw pain of grief.

The problem is that numbness tends to block *all* feelings — desirable, as well as undesirable. So you might not feel as much pain, but you also can't feel happiness or hope. The world seems empty, so you go through the motions, just getting by with daily responsibilities. Numbness can be hidden, and some might misinterpret your demeanor for healing or stoicism, believing you're competently managing your grief — when you are, in fact, emotionally stuck.

Do This

Journaling can help you understand your numbness and use it as a bridge to begin feeling again — to whatever degree you're ready for. The prompts in this section can assist you in understanding how numbness benefits you and to decide when you're ready to begin processing your emotions again.

Prompt 1

Think about the cause of your grief (your loss) and the effects of numbness in your daily life — how you go about your day-to-day interactions and responsibilities. What does your numbness protect you from? Write about the positive aspects of not having to feel emotions in the way that you would normally.

_____

_____

_____

_____

_____

_____

_____

_____

_____

Prompt 2

Focus on your body by bringing your attention to your breath. For a few minutes, breathe slowly and deeply, feeling the breath while it moves in and out of your nose, your throat, your lungs.

When you're ready, close your eyes and shift your attention to your heart region, and then into your belly. See whether you can identify where the sense of numbness exists in your body.

Visualize that numbness as a cocoon spun around your emotions and keeping them safe. What emotions are sleeping within that cocoon?

When you're ready, open your eyes and journal about the emotions that you saw within the cocoon.

_____

_____

_____

_____

_____

_____

_____

_____

_____

_____

_____

_____

_____

_____

_____

_____

_____

_____

_____

Prompt 3

This prompt builds on what you write for Prompt 2.

Repeat the breath meditation at the start of Prompt 2 and visualize the cocoon again.

This time, imagine the emotions within the cocoon beginning to stir and move and stretch the cocoon's walls. Imagine the cocoon gently opening, peeling back to allow the emotions to emerge one by one.

However, you have the power to decide which emotions can come out and which ones must stay within the cocoon.

Which emotions will you allow out and why?

_____

_____

_____

_____

_____

_____

_____

_____

_____

_____

_____

Which emotions will you keep in the cocoon and why?

_____

_____

_____

_____

_____

_____

_____

_____

_____

TIP

After you decide to allow one or more emotions to emerge from the cocoon, I recommend journaling to Prompt 2 in the "Acknowledging and Validating Your Feelings" section, earlier in this chapter.

Taking Action Against Loneliness

Loneliness is another part of grief that isn't recognized often enough. In this state of grief, it can seem like no one really understands what you're going through, and everyone's responses, no matter how kindly intended, fall short.

Even when you're surrounded by supportive friends and family, it's possible to feel completely alone. In addition, loneliness is often coupled with depression, which can cause you to disconnect from and even push away people who want to help you.

This kind of loneliness, if it continues too long, has been shown to be destructive to your physical health, making you prone to illness by suppressing the immune system and increasing risk of cardiovascular disease. The good news is that you *can* overcome your loneliness, with honesty, conscious effort on your part, and help from your support group.

Do This

The journaling prompts in this section are each followed by an action that you can take to help you overcome your loneliness. You can respond to any of the prompts that appeal to you and in any order.

Prompt 1

Set a timer for five minutes and write about your feeling of loneliness and how your loneliness affects your life. For example, are you refusing others' offers of help and pushing them away? Are you hiding in corners alone whenever you're with a group of people? Are you staying home and sleeping more? Write about what's true for you.

_____

_____

_____

_____

_____

_____

_____

_____

_____

_____

_____

_____

_____

_____

_____

_____

_____

_____

_____

_____

_____

_____

_____

When you're ready to take action, choose someone whom you're comfortable with and tell them how you're feeling. Explain how your behaviors are influenced by your sense of loneliness and ask them to help you to reconnect with others. Include a discussion about what kinds of connection you're ready for — for example, individuals or small private gatherings versus public gatherings or larger groups. The following prompt can help you determine what types of connections you'd like to make.

Prompt 2

Brainstorm a step that you can take on your own to reconnect with other people. Start by making a list of people you want to connect with, social events you might want to attend, grief support groups you can join, and so on. Include possibilities that you feel ready to try, as well as ones that you don't.

_____

_____

_____

_____

_____

_____

_____

_____

_____

_____

Choose the easiest one of the action items you brainstormed and put it on your calendar to do this week. For example, if you wrote down your sister's name as someone to reconnect with, make a date to get together for lunch or a walk.

Prompt 3

Helping others is an effective way to get outside out of your own thoughts and emotions, makes you feel good, and puts your loss into a broader perspective.

List five local organizations or events that you would feel good to be a part of.

_____

_____

_____

_____

_____

When you're ready to take action, choose one of the organizations or events that you wrote down and make arrangements to volunteer for something that feels doable for you.

REMEMBER

Be understanding and kind to yourself — you're doing the best that you can. Loneliness may be a part of grief, but you're not actually alone, and the feelings of loneliness you're experiencing won't be with you forever. Make the effort to reach out to others. You might be surprised by their responses.

Getting Past Guilt

On top of all the other painful emotions that grief brings with it, guilt might be the most devious. It comes in several forms and sometimes piles the different forms one on top of the other. And although people might tell you (or you might tell yourself) that nothing is your fault and you shouldn't feel guilty, feelings of guilt aren't going to go away just because you tell them to.

Identifying types of guilt associated with grief

There are three basic kinds of guilt associated with loss. You might feel any of these guilt types alone or in combination with one or more of the others:

>> **Survivor's guilt:** This type of guilt usually occurs when something bad, such as death or injury, has happened to someone else and you feel you didn't deserve to be spared or that you should have been the one that it happened to.

>> **I-should-have-known-better-or-done-more guilt:** This guilt attacks you when you feel directly or indirectly responsible for the misfortune of someone else. You blame yourself for what happened, even though, logically, you know it wasn't your fault.

>> **Feelings-of-selfishness guilt:** This guilt may haunt you when you lose something you believe you shouldn't have wanted in the first place.

For example, if you experienced the loss of a dream of having or becoming something (a beautiful home, great career, famous artist, and so on) because of illness or some other life event, you may feel that it was selfish of you to have that dream in the first place. You think you don't deserve to grieve, so your grief is compounded by simply having the feelings that you do.

The prompts in the following section are designed to help you become aware of negative self-talk, understand the type of guilt you're feeling, and find ways to turn guilt into an opportunity to take positive action.

Journaling for awareness

Using guided journaling prompts can improve your understanding of the different kinds of guilt associated with grief and
increase self-awareness of your guilt.

Do This

The prompts that follow are designed to help you become aware of
negative self-talk and understand the type of guilt you're feeling.

Prompt 1

Do any of the guilt-type descriptions in the preceding section
apply to you? If so, which one(s), and how does that guilt affect
your ability to accept your loss?

_____

_____

_____

_____

_____

_____

Prompt 2

What repetitive self-talk accompanies your feelings of guilt?
For example, you might be saying over and over in your mind,
"It's my fault this happened." Write an opposing statement
that you can use to counter the negative self-talk, such as, "It's
not my fault this happened."

TIP

If you find that you can't believe the opposing statement, soften
it by adding "I want . . ." at the beginning. Using the preceding
example, you could write, "I don't want it to be my fault this
happened." Progress comes in baby steps.

_____

_____

_____

_____

_____

_____

Prompt 3

Do you think your feelings of guilt are warranted or unwarranted?

If warranted, write about what you did and what you need to do in order to forgive yourself. For example, you might make amends by volunteering for a related worthy cause, perhaps helping others to avoid a similar mistake.

If unwarranted, write two positive statements that you can repeat to yourself to balance the negative guilt self-talk. You can start with, "My guilt is unwarranted because . . ."

_____

_____

_____

_____

_____

_____

_____

Journaling for transformation

Emotion is simply energy that resides in your body. And because emotion is energy, it can be transformed and the energy expressed or used in many ways. The key to transforming unwanted emotional energy to a positive force is first, to be aware of the emotion and its energy, and, second, determine how you want that energy to be expressed.

Do This

To explore two different ways to transform guilt, respond to either or both of the following prompts.

Prompt 1

Close your eyes and hold your hands in front of yourself, palms up. Imagine that your guilt lies in the palm of your left hand as a ball of energy. Visualize the energy: Is it dark or light, opaque or transparent, and does it pulse or vibrate? When you can visualize and feel that ball of guilt energy, imagine the energy traveling from your left palm to your right palm. As it travels, it transforms into a positive emotion — changing color, becoming lighter, vibrating faster, and reforming itself into a ball in your right palm. What emotion is now in your right hand?

Write down the name of the emotion. In what way(s) could you use this positive emotional energy to benefit yourself or others?

_____

_____

_____

_____

_____

Prompt 2

Releasing emotional energy into the elements, where it disperses, is another way to transform the emotion. Create a brief ritual or ceremony to release your guilt. One way to do this is by writing your guilt-thoughts on paper and then burning the paper. Journal about how you feel after the ceremony.

_____

_____

_____

_____

_____

_____

_____

_____

_____

Journaling After Losing Someone You Love

Grief is messy and unpredictable. And sometimes, even after you think you've gotten through the worst of it, it shows up again in full force. When you've lost someone you love through death, divorce, or another event, anniversaries, holidays, and other calendar-based reminders of that person can make you feel like you're back at the beginning. As a result, you might be tempted to isolate yourself by withdrawing from other people and activities during those times.

That's why it's important to recognize in advance that you will have to face periods that are just plain difficult to get through.

TIP

In my experience, the best way to manage those hard times is to remember the good ones. Focusing on the fond memories and characteristics of the person you lost doesn't take your pain away, but it does change the intensity of your emotion and may shift it entirely.

Whenever you find yourself painfully reminded of your loss, select one of the following prompts and journal about it.

> ❯❯ Write a letter to your loved one and tell them about the quirks and endearing qualities you loved most about them.

>> Write the story of a particular date or holiday you had together that stands out. Begin with, "One time . . ."

>> Complete the following sentence, starting with the name of the person: "[Name] used to make me laugh when . . ."

>> Create an altar that displays a few of their favorite things on it or a picture. Light a candle and journal about the good times you used to have together.

>> Go to a place you used to enjoy being together, sit quietly for a bit, and then free-write for 20 minutes about what you're feeling.

>> Ask your friends to each write something about a special memory they had with your loved one. Collect these stories without reading them and put them in a jar or other container. Whenever you're feeling sad about your loss, take out one of the stories and read it. Journal about how the story makes you feel and the memories it brings up.

REMEMBER

It's okay to find yourself smiling or laughing when you remember your loved one. Feelings of happiness and joy don't lessen how much you miss them and wish they were with you during those anniversaries and holidays. Remembering the good times is part of the healing process. And take to heart that if that person was with you right now, they would most likely be laughing, as well.

Chapter **15**

Transforming Relationships

Relationships form a core part of every person's life. Starting with the family caring for you from birth and expanding to neighbors, friends, teachers, bosses, co-workers, lovers, and acquaintances, every relationship leaves its mark on your life — influencing your beliefs, attitudes, and world view. You could even say that the relationships that you don't get to choose (family, teachers, and so on) influence who you become, and you define yourself by the relationships that you do choose (friends, lovers, spouses).

Relationships can be beneficial or destructive — and sometimes, both. And they're complex. Any time you mix together two people who inevitably have different genetic makeup, histories, and communication styles, you're bound to discover ways you fit smoothly together and ways that cause friction between you.

Because relationships are so vital, it's worthwhile to use journaling to consider the people in your life and gain awareness of which relationships are working for you and which ones aren't. Journaling can help you determine which bonds to release and which to strengthen. And journaling can help you determine ways to do both.

Prioritizing Your Relationship with Yourself

Before examining your relationships with others, it can be beneficial to take a look at what is perhaps the most important relationship of all — the one with yourself. The way you relate to yourself is the foundation of every other relationship. And if this relationship is unhealthy, it adversely affects all relationships in your life.

It's possible that you've never nurtured this vital relationship, never thought about it quite this way before. Yet it began when you were a child in how others saw and treated you.

Carrying around negative feelings about yourself affects your physical, mental, and emotional health negatively and can manifest as unhappiness, guilt, or self-loathing. On the other hand, having a positive, healthy self-relationship keeps you physically, mentally, and emotionally healthy, and you're more likely to have strong relationships with others.

For these reasons, it's important to reflect on this most vital of all relationships.

Do This

Use the following journaling prompts to explore your self-relationship and what it takes to have a strong relationship with the one person you always have in your life: you.

For the deepest insights into how you relate to and care for yourself, respond to all of the prompts. You can do so in any order you wish.

Prompt 1

Describe yourself in the third-person, as if through someone else's eyes. What are your best qualities? What are your strengths and how do you shine in that person's eyes?

_____

_____

_____

_____

_____

_____

_____

_____

_____

_____

How do you feel after seeing your strengths as if someone else is describing them?

_____

_____

Brainstorm ways you can focus on these strengths in your daily life, in the way you think about yourself and in your interactions with others.

_____

_____

_____

_____

_____

_____

Prompt 2

In what ways do you take good care of yourself physically and emotionally? Brainstorm a list of actions that you can take to expand upon or improve these ways you take care of yourself.

_____

_____

_____

_____

_____

_____

_____

_____

Prompt 3

In what ways do you neglect yourself? Brainstorm a list of actions you can take to improve your self-care.

_____

_____

_____

_____

_____

_____

_____

_____

Prompt 4

How comfortable are you when you're alone? Follow these instructions to make a creative cluster for the concept of being alone. (Discover more about how to use creative clusters, along with an illustration of a completed cluster, in Chapter 10.)

1. **Write the words *being alone* in the center of the space provided and circle it.**

This is the nucleus.

2. **Write whatever associated words come to mind.**

Let the writing radiate outward from the center.

3. **Draw a circle around each word or phrase.**

Don't think too long or analyze, just keep letting those associations flow.

4. **Continue writing associations and ideas triggered by your nucleus for a minute or two.**

What themes, images, and emotions surfaced in your creative cluster? What did you discover about being alone with yourself through this exercise?

_____

_____

_____

_____

_____

_____

_____

_____

For Better or Worse: Examining Your Relationships with Others

Typically, when someone mentions being "in a relationship," they're referring to a romantic relationship, meaning dating, partnership, or marriage. But life is full of many types of relationships, and each type has its own unique rewards and challenges.

In this section, you can use journaling to explore how you define your relationships by first categorizing the people in your life into different types of relationships. Second, you consider which of these relationships are most rewarding and which are the most challenging. These prompts can help you begin thinking about all the people and different relationship functions in your life, as well as what makes a relationship rewarding or challenging.

Do This

For best results, respond to all the prompts in this section in order.

Prompt 1

List the people in your life according to relationship type. I provide the most common types of relationships in the following list. Below each type, write the names of people in your life — both welcome and unwelcome — who fit into that category. Completing this activity raises awareness of the many people you have relationships with in your life, as well as in which categories most of your relationships are concentrated. Listing everyone can also remind you of people you might not automatically include when you think of relationships.

» **Family of origin:** Parents/guardians, step-parents, siblings. Generally, the people with whom you grew up and whom you generally include when you talk about your family.

_____

_____

_____

» **Extended family:** Grandparents, aunts, uncles, cousins, and so on. You may not have had a lot of contact with some extended family members, so list here only the ones who influence (or have influenced) your life.

_____

_____

_____

» **Offspring:** Children and grandchildren.

_____

_____

_____

» **Romantic and sexual:** People you date on a regular basis, casual sexual partners, domestic partners, spouses.

_____

_____

» **Friendship:** People you feel close enough to share intimate details with and whom you know you could depend on in time of need (and vice versa).

_____

_____

_____

_____

>> **Professional:** Work or professional relationships of any kind.

_____

_____

_____

_____

>> **Community and social groups:** People you interface with only within the context of a particular community or common interest group.

_____

_____

_____

_____

>> **Acquaintances:** People you're friendly with and see on an occasional basis, but whom you don't feel as close with as friends.

_____

_____

_____

_____

Prompt 2

Of the people and types of relationships you listed in Prompt 1, identify your most rewarding relationship and why you consider it so. For example, you might consider your most rewarding relationship to be with a partner, child, or best friend. Write that person's name and then why that relationship is most rewarding to you.

My most rewarding relationship is with _____

because _____

_____

_____

_____

_____

_____

_____

Next, write the name of the person whom you feel most challenged by and what makes that relationship so difficult. (And yes, it's possible that the same person fits both roles.)

My most challenging relationship is with _____

because _____

_____

_____

_____

_____

_____

_____

Prompt 3

Write about whether and how the relationships you identified in Prompt 2 have evolved. Consider the differences between what those relationships were like in the beginning and how they are now. In particular, think about your role and influence: How have your attitude and behaviors affected the nature of these relationships?

Has the rewarding relationship always been that way, or has it gotten better over time? If it shifted, in what ways have you changed and in what ways has the other person changed?

_____

_____

_____

_____

_____

_____

_____

Has the challenging relationship always been difficult, or has it gotten worse over time? If it shifted, in what ways have you changed and in what ways has the other person changed?

_____

_____

_____

_____

_____

_____

_____

Prompt 4

Reflect on your answers to Prompts 1 through 3. Then journal for a few minutes about the following questions and any other insights that came up for you while considering your impactful relationships.

Here are a few questions to consider as you journal about your relationships. You don't need to answer all of the questions — select those that you find most thought-provoking.

>> Were you surprised by how many people you have relationships with or in what categories you placed some of them in Prompt 1?

>> Thinking about the rewarding relationship you identified in Prompt 2, what qualities of that connection are shared with other rewarding relationships? For example, is shared values important for a rewarding relationship? Which qualities are significant to you?

>> Thinking about the challenging relationship you identified in Prompt 2, and other difficult relationships you've had, what qualities do you think make these relationships challenging? For example, does conflict make a relationship challenging or is that part of any relationship?

>> How did the ways you've changed over time from Prompt 3 influence the direction of those relationships?

>> What's your biggest takeaway from examining your relationships through journaling?

_____

_____

_____

_____

_____

_____

_____

_____

_____

_____

_____

_____

_____

_____

_____

_____

_____

_____

Finding Empathy

Empathy, the ability to understand the feelings and experiences of others, is an important quality for any relationship — particularly, for challenging relationships. When you understand how another person is feeling, you're better able to respond in a way that makes that person feel seen and heard. They feel less alone and more supported. Paired with _compassion_ — a desire to alleviate others' pain and distress — empathy prompts you to take action to help others and de-escalate tense emotional interactions.

The journaling prompts in this section can help you recognize the important role empathy plays in your rewarding relationships and find empathy for those people with whom you have difficult relationships.

Do This

Select two or more of the following prompts to respond to. They can be done in any order.

Prompt 1

Think about a time in a rewarding relationship where you felt empathy for the other person. How did you know you were feeling empathy, and what actions did your empathy prompt you to take? How did that person respond? And how did their response make you feel? For example, perhaps you helped them feel more comfortable in an awkward social situation and they later thanked you.

_____

_____

_____

_____

_____

_____

_____

_____

_____

_____

Prompt 2

Think about a person with whom you have a difficult or challenging relationship. Now, remember a time when you had a disagreement or upsetting interaction. Put yourself in the other person's shoes and write about what happened from *their* perspective. Be sure to imagine, as honestly as possible, how they understood the situation and why they responded the way they did, including how they might have interpreted your voice and behaviors.

_____

_____

_____

_____

_____

_____

_____

_____

_____

_____

_____

_____

_____

_____

_____

How did writing about the disagreement from their perspective affect your ability to empathize with the other person?

_____

_____

_____

_____

Prompt 3

Recall a time when someone said something that hurt your feelings. Now, think about the challenges they were facing at the time. For example, were they not feeling well or experiencing issues at work, and did they lose self-control because of whatever was going on? How does trying to understand their challenges affect your feelings about the interaction? Write your response in the space provided.

_____

_____

_____

_____

_____

_____

_____

_____

_____

Prompt 4

How do you know when someone is empathizing with you, and how does empathy help you? Does it help you feel less alone or comforted, for example? Which of their empathizing behaviors could you adopt and use when empathizing with someone else?

_____

_____

_____

_____

_____

_____

_____

_____

_____

_____

Enhancing Romantic Partnerships

Someone once told me that the way to create a stable and fulfilling relationship is to "find out what the other person wants and give it to them." And in my own experience, I have found this to be true. (Of course, this works best when the other person responds in kind. Otherwise, you have a lopsided relationship in which one person is always giving and the other taking.)

The core idea in that statement is that healthy, loving partnerships include attentiveness, respect, support, and trust. But over time, it's easy to take the things you used to love about your partner for granted and to allow the daily habits that annoy you to take center stage. To complicate matters, communication differences can derail attempts that you make to have constructive conversations with your partner.

Journaling about your most intimate relationship can make a difference in how you perceive and communicate effectively with your partner. Writing about your feelings increases your awareness of how you respond in different situations, and it helps you see what you and your partner each need to feel loved and supported. It can also help you change the way you approach important discussions.

WARNING

It's also important to understand that it takes two people to build and maintain a healthy partnership. If the other person is not interested or engaged in working to improve your relationship, sabotages your efforts, is emotionally or physically abusive, or trust between you has been lost for other reasons, the relationship is unhealthy (or even toxic). In this case, it may be best for your own safety and emotional health to get some professional counseling and possibly leave the relationship. The journaling guidance in this section is geared toward helping to improve relationships that are already relatively healthy or could simply use a little boost.

The following journaling prompts are designed to help you reawaken and remember your partner's characteristics that you fell in love with and to create ways to work through communication differences.

Do This

Respond to any or all of the following prompts that appeal to you. That said, I recommend doing Prompts 7 and 8 together, as they both explore the topic of communication styles.

Prompt 1

List all the positive traits you can think of for your partner. When you're done, review the list and circle the traits that first drew you to them. Remembering the traits that first drew you together can help revive some of those early romantic feelings and also remind you to consciously look for and appreciate those traits in your partner.

_____

_____

_____

_____

_____

_____

_____

_____

Prompt 2

Write the story of how you met and how you fell in love. What do you think attracted you most to each other? And what are you most grateful for in the relationship? You can use this prompt to build on your response to the previous prompt, though it can also stand by itself. Telling the story of how you fell in love can help you remember aspects of your partner that you've come to take for granted over time and help you renew your appreciation and gratitude for the positive things in your relationship.

_____

_____

_____

_____

_____

_____

_____

_____

_____

_____

_____

_____

_____

Prompt 3

This three-part prompt helps you focus on the ways in which you and your partner fulfill each other's needs for love, emotional support, and acknowledgment. In addition, it asks you to consider actions you can take to improve your role in this aspect of your relationship.

What things does your partner do that help you feel loved, supported, and appreciated?

_____

_____

_____

_____

_____

_____

What things do you do to help your partner feel loved, supported, and appreciated?

_____

_____

_____

_____

_____

_____

_____

What is one thing you could do today to help your partner feel more loved and appreciated?

_____

_____

_____

Prompt 4

Research has shown that sexual closeness builds and maintains feelings of love. If you're intimate with your current partner, how do you feel about your sexual relationship and why? What steps can you take to improve that part of your relationship?

_____

_____

_____

_____

_____

_____

_____

_____

Prompt 5

What traumas or past hurts get reactivated in you when you and your partner argue? What do you need from them so that you feel supported and safe when this reactivation happens?

For example, if you had parents who were critical of your efforts and it seemed like nothing you did was ever good enough, whenever your partner questions something you've done it triggers those old feelings and you tend to become defensive, even though your partner's question may be coming from a place of curiosity or a desire to be constructive. What would you need your partner to do or say in order to help you understand their true intention and hear the question without feeling defensive?

_____

_____

_____

_____

_____

_____

_____

_____

Prompt 6

What traumas and past hurts get reactivated in your partner during arguments? What do they need from you so that they feel supported and safe when this reactivation happens? (See the instructions in Prompt 5 for an example of how a hurt or trauma can be reactivated.)

TIP

If you don't know what your partner needs when they're feeling triggered, use this space to brainstorm ways to start a conversation (during a calm time) so that you can find out.

_____

_____

_____

_____

_____

_____

_____

_____

_____

Prompt 7

Describe your and your partner's communication styles and the differences between them. For example, which one of you is more willing to talk about feelings and/or pursue a resolution to an issue? And which one of you is most likely to bottle up their feelings?

_____

_____

_____

_____

_____

_____

_____

_____

How do your communication differences affect your day-to-day interactions, and what could you do to accommodate those differences?

_____

_____

_____

_____

_____

Prompt 8

Brainstorm ways to find out more about each other's communication styles and how to improve your overall communication.

_____

_____

_____

_____

_____

Improving Family Relationships

Among the family you grew up with — your *family of origin* — you developed your core beliefs about life and all it entails. It's when you gained your first awareness of self. As a result, your family had a major influence on who you've become and how you relate to others.

If you had your physical and emotional needs met and felt safe, supported, and loved, you probably grew up with a strong sense of self. But if any of those important aspects of love and safety were missing from your upbringing, you developed natural defensive mechanisms that helped you survive family deficits and dysfunctions. And you likely unconsciously incorporated those mechanisms into patterns of behavior that, though they served you when you were young, don't necessarily serve your adult relationships.

Like it or not, we carry the problem baggage of our families — and our problem relationships with members of our families — throughout our lives.

The following prompts help you process how family baggage affects your ongoing relationships with your family, as well as those outside your family. The increased awareness can assist you in figuring out ways to strengthen your already strong family relationships and build up the weak ones.

Do This

Use Prompts 1 through 5 to help you write about and process your complicated family relationships. Not all prompts apply to your situation, so select the ones that resonate most for you. Then reflect on these responses in Prompt 6.

Note: The following prompts refer to your "parents," meaning those people who actually raised and parented you, whether those were your biological parent(s), adoptive parents, family members, or other primary caregivers.

Prompt 1

How old were your parents when you became part of the family, and where were they in their own development as adults? How do you think this affected their attitudes toward parenting?

_____

_____

_____

_____

_____

_____

_____

Prompt 2

In what ways did your parents make you feel loved or unloved? What behaviors and words did they use, and how did this affect your sense of self?

_____

_____

_____

_____

_____

_____

_____

Prompt 3

What object or metaphor best represents your feelings toward your family, including parents, siblings, and anyone else you grew up with?

_____

_____

_____

_____

_____

_____

Prompt 4

What was the best or most useful lesson you learned from your family, including parents, siblings, and anyone else you grew up with?

_____

_____

_____

_____

_____

_____

_____

Prompt 5

Follow these directions to make a creative cluster in the space provided (you can find detailed directions for creative clustering in Chapter 10, along with an example of a completed cluster).

1. **Write the name of one of your parents or siblings in the center of the space provided and circle it.**

   This is the nucleus.

2. **Write whatever associated words come to mind.**

   Let the writing radiate outward from the center.

3. **Draw a circle around each word or phrase.**

   Don't think too long or analyze, just keep letting those
   associations flow.

4. **Continue writing associations and ideas triggered by your
   nucleus for a minute or two.**

Write a poem incorporating the words and phrases from your
cluster (you don't have to include all of them). It can be a poem
about your parent or sibling, or it can be a poem inspired by the
associated thoughts and ideas you wrote around the nucleus.

This poem is just for you, so don't worry if it's not a master-
piece. Writing poetry inspired from your creative cluster can
help you gain insights and/or clarity about your associated
thoughts.

Prompt 6

Review and reflect on what you wrote in response to your selected prompts and consider the following questions:

>> What recurring themes or images come up in your prompt responses, and what insights can you gain from them?

>> What have you discovered about yourself by writing about your family?

>> What attitudes and behaviors toward your family do you want to change and what are some of the steps you could take to make those changes?

_____

_____

_____

_____

_____

_____

_____

_____

_____

_____

_____

_____

_____

_____

_____

_____

_____

_____

_____

_____

_____

_____

Deepening Friendships

Adult friendships are different in many ways from those you had when you were a child. Even the friendships with people whom you've known since grade school have changed over time. Yet having healthy adult friendships is as important to your mental/ emotional well-being as it was for you when you were young. Quality friendships protect you from stress, anxiety, and depression and are especially beneficial later in life.

That said, building and maintaining adult friendships can be challenging. The time and energy we used to have to nurture friendships gets co-opted by adult responsibilities and shifting priorities.

Journaling reflectively (which you can read about in Chapter 5) about what friendship means for you personally and the quality of relationships with the people you spend your time with can clarify what you want most from your friendships and what you need to do to make them better.

In the prompts that follow, you can explore your beliefs about friendship, discover what you appreciate most about your friends, and find more ways to nurture friendships.

Do This

Respond to any or all of the following journaling prompts that resonate for you.

Prompt 1

To identify your underlying beliefs about friendship, describe the qualities you believe are important to a good friendship.

_____

_____

_____

_____

_____

_____

_____

Read what you wrote and circle any beliefs that you have about friendship — any *shoulds* and *have-tos*. Review each of these statements and ask yourself, "Is this 100 percent true?" For example, if you wrote "good friends are loyal," do you believe that loyalty is 100 percent necessary for a good friendship? Write about how you feel and what you notice about your beliefs when you question these statements. Perhaps questioning makes you feel defensive, or maybe you notice that some beliefs are stronger than others.

_____

_____

_____

_____

_____

_____

Prompt 2

Think about the people you choose to spend your time with most often. What are their best qualities? Write your answers in the space provided.

TIP

Follow up this journaling activity by letting them know how much you appreciate them and their friendship.

_____

_____

_____

_____

_____

_____

_____

_____

_____

_____

_____

_____

Prompt 3

Think about the kinds of things you do to nurture your friendships. Do you feel you need to do more? If so, what actions could you take? Make a list here and then begin doing some of these actions when you interact with your friends. As you do, notice how your friends respond. Continue with those actions or behaviors that seem to nurture or improve your friendships.

_____

_____

_____

_____

_____

_____

_____

The Part of Tens

IN THIS PART . . .

Find tips that can help you maintain a rich and thriving journaling practice.

Generate your own journaling prompts so that you can deepen your inner exploration or explore any life situation — or just for fun.

Chapter **16**

Ten Tips to Maintain a Vibrant Journaling Practice

Journaling is easy to start, but like anything new, it takes time to become integrated into your life. New routines take intentional action to stick and become habits. The first five tips in this chapter can help you start and maintain a long-term practice of journaling.

Another aspect of sustaining a rich and vibrant journaling practice is ensuring that you're being rewarded for your efforts — that you're experiencing a greater sense of well-being, self-awareness, and insights about life and relationships. Whenever you start to feel like your practice is becoming dry or that you're just not getting what you want out of it, try one or more of the last five tips, which are guaranteed to revitalize your enthusiasm for journaling.

Stay True to Your Purpose

Acknowledge your motivations for journaling and have a purpose or topic in mind each time you sit down to write. If you're not sure of your purpose, review Chapter 2, which covers many benefits and reasons for journaling.

Whatever your primary reasons for journaling — whether you want to record and process daily events and emotions, improve your overall sense of well-being, analyze and heal from trauma, or be better organized — regularly remind yourself of your motivations. Doing so will provide the impetus and energy you need to keep going back to your journal time and time again.

In addition, have a specific goal for each journaling session. This direction can help you get engaged and stay focused. There's nothing wrong with sitting down to write without knowing what you want to write about — sometimes, that's just the way it is — but you can find focus faster and dig more deeply into what matters when you know what you want from your session.

See Yourself as a Journal Writer

Studies have shown that we succeed at things we identify ourselves with — and fail at those we don't.

If you see yourself as the type of person who enjoys journaling and who keeps a journal consistently, then you will play out that role in your life and be successful at journaling regularly. When you identify as a journal writer, journaling becomes part of who you *are*, and therefore, it becomes a priority for you.

Conversely, if you see yourself as undisciplined, someone who doesn't like to write, or someone who's afraid of being honest with yourself, you're more likely to experience journaling as difficult and not carry through on your intentions.

It's simple: The more deeply you identify with the image of yourself as a journal writer, the more motivated you become to keep your journal. Not sure how you see yourself? Sit down with your journal to explore this topic.

Start Small

Like with any new habit, it's best to start small with journaling. For example, if your goal is to write 30 minutes per day, schedule just 10 minutes to start. If that's too much, then go for five. You'd be surprised by how much you can do in five minutes!

After you successfully journal for 10 minutes daily for a week, increase the amount to 15 minutes. Continue in this way until you've increased your time to meet your goal.

By setting a low-commitment expectation, you're more likely to sit down and do it. After all, what excuse can you make for not setting aside five minutes to do something so important to you?

Make It Easy

Habits are simpler to form when they're easy. Here are a few actions you can take to make regular journaling stress-free:

>> **Set up an attractive and comfortable journaling space.** Make it a space that you *want* to spend time in — anything from a home office to a cozy cushion for writing in bed.

>> **Make sure your journaling tools are within easy reach.** Place your pen or pencil, drawing tools, and notebook or computer nearby. (If you want to protect your journal from prying eyes, consider a locking drawer or small safe near where you like to write.)

>> **Pair journaling with something else you like to do that's already part of your routine.** For example, if you already practice a musical instrument on a regular basis, journal *before* you play your instrument and make music your reward.

Be Flexible

Even after you establish a regular journaling habit (flip to Chapter 4 for the how-to's on setting yourself up for journaling), life happens. When the unexpected hijacks your day or your week, allow yourself to flex. When possible, journal at a different time of day or write just a few lines on the go. But if you can't journal at all, don't worry about it or berate yourself. Simply start again as soon as possible.

WARNING

With flexibility comes a caution: Don't allow yourself to fall prey to inertia and *out* of the habit of journaling. If that happens, go back to the beginning. Remind yourself of your reasons for journaling and start small to reestablish your journaling practice.

Be Honest

When you write, remember that you're writing only for yourself. Be honest with yourself. Don't judge or censor your writing. Express what you're thinking and feeling, and don't avoid the difficult topics. You gain the most from your journaling when you're open and honest with yourself.

Use Journaling Prompts

When you're stuck for what to write about, use journaling prompts to prime your creative pump. After you begin with a prompt, allow yourself to go wherever it leads you. You can also build on a prompt by asking topic-related questions to help dig deeply into the prompt's subject. I give some tips for creating or finding good writing prompts in Chapter 17.

Change Things Up

If you journal at the same time and in the same way every day, you might find yourself getting bored with the practice. If you get into a journaling rut, try changing your method, schedule, or both to reawaken your journaling inspiration.

For example, for a long time, I always journaled right after I woke each morning. However, after a while my journaling seemed shallow — I wasn't delving into any important topics, I was writing about the same things day after day, and I wasn't gaining any new insights about myself. (Yawn.) The solution, for me, was to switch things up by writing before bed for a while.

Alternatively, I could have switched from reflective journaling (introduced in Chapter 5) to mindfulness journaling (which I talk about in Chapter 6) or gratitude journaling (discussed in Chapter 9) to reinvigorate my mind for a few weeks before returning to my regular practice.

Pair Up with a Writing Partner

Sometimes, you need to make a commitment to someone else for that added boost to your motivation. A tried-and-true method of ensuring accountability for beginning and maintaining a practice — and having fun in the process — is a journaling partner (flip back to Chapter 4 for details).

When you have a partner, it's easier to stick with your commitment. You can share your journal entries with each other (or not), give each other feedback, encourage each other to keep going when you feel discouraged, and even journal together at the same time.

Make it Fun

Remember to have fun while you're journaling. Sometimes, you work through topics or situations that are quite serious and even painful. No one's life is free from chaos or hurt. These situations are what your journal is all about, but balance these heavier journaling sessions with lighter topics and techniques. Here are a few ideas for making your journaling whimsical and fun:

>> Use play to enhance your creative skills (see Chapter 8).

>> Do a web search for *whimsical journaling prompts* to find lighter topics to write about.

>> Start a new notebook, write in color, or turn your notebook upside down for an entry.

>> Pick a beloved object and write about how it came to be yours.

Whenever you feel like your journaling has become a chore or you're tired of dealing with serious topics, remember that fun is the key to making it fresh again.

Chapter **17**

Ten Ways to Generate Inspiring Journaling Prompts

E veryone needs a little journaling inspiration from time to time, and what better source of inspiration than prompts?

All journaling methods can benefit from using prompts that align with the method's purpose. For example, if you're engaged in reflective journaling, you likely want to use a prompt that helps you think deeply about your attitudes and responses. For creative journaling, you may want one that encourages visual expression, and so on.

The problem is finding prompts that fit with your journaling type *and* are meaningful enough to help you on your personal development journey. Generic prompts, such as, "What's your favorite color?" may not meet your criteria for *meaningful*.

That's one reason why I recommend generating your own prompts whenever possible. In addition to generally being more evocative, writing your own prompts boosts your creativity, assists your quest for self-knowledge, and is just plain fun.

Following are ten different methods for creating unique prompts relevant to you and your situation. Whenever you're stuck for what to journal about, give one of these methods a try.

Use Current Events

Scroll through online news or read a newspaper or magazine until you find a topic that interests you. Depending on your goal, search for a headline that generates a strong emotional reaction, appeals to your whimsical side, or simply makes you think and reflect on your own life. If you want to avoid politics and financial news, peruse your local news for feel-good stories. The entertainment section and even the comics can also be good sources for journaling prompts.

Keep Lists

Make it a habit to keep lists of journaling topics when they occur to you outside of your normal journaling time. Issues, problems, random thoughts, plans for the future, things that bring you joy — these are all fodder for journaling.

For example, maybe you want to take a Mediterranean cruise. List all the questions you have about cruising and the countries you want to see. Ask yourself questions such as, "What am I most excited about seeing and why?" and "What activities does the cruise offer, which ones appeal to me most, and why?" These questions can be fun, help you clarify what you want to get out of your travels, and reveal underlying thoughts and emotions.

Browse Blogs and Friends' Social Media Posts

Generate topic ideas by reading blogs and social media posts written by people you know or follow online. You can journal responses to their posts or reflect on how those topics affect you personally. Ask questions and explore opposing arguments. Or venture into the Comments section and use a fellow reader's response as a starting point for your journaling.

Use Images

A picture is worth a thousand words — or can be, when you journal about it. Open a family photo album or browse older pictures on your smartphone until you find one that intrigues you.

Write a story about how that picture was taken, who was in it, and why they were together. Describe the background and what people are wearing. If there are no people in the picture, describe the scene and why the picture speaks to you.

What memories and emotions does the picture evoke for you? Explore these and any related associations that come up while you're writing.

Pick a Word or Phrase from a Book

This is one of the easiest and most random ways to generate a writing prompt. Simple grab any book off your shelf, close your eyes, open the book to a random page, and point your finger anywhere on the page. Open your eyes and write about the word or phrase that your finger is pointing at. Chapter 8 talks about this journaling method more in depth.

Explore Extremes

Want to know more about yourself? Think up extreme questions using words such as *greatest, most, best, worst,* and so on. Here are a few examples:

>> What's your greatest fear?

>> What's your best memory?

>> Who's the worst person you know?

>> What's your least favorite activity and why?

What is the most extreme question you can think of?

Examine Your Values

Write a list of values that you hold dear in your life and then ask questions about each of them.

For example, if you wrote *authenticity,* you could ask questions such as, "What is authenticity and how is it expressed in my life?" to clarify what you mean and where it fits into how you live.

Ask questions using the 5Ws+1H technique (see Chapter 5 for more details about this technique), which has you start with Who, What, Where, When, Why, and How. Create questions such as, "What does [value] mean to me?"; "What happens when [value] isn't present in my life?"; and "When did I first begin to appreciate the importance of [value]?"

Picture the Impossible

Do you love fantasy or science fiction? Picturing the impossible is a great way to get your creative juices flowing and have fun at the same time, while finding out more about how your mind works.

For example, imagine you could have a superpower. Which superpower would you want and why? How would that power help the world — or would it?

Allow yourself to bring fantasies from your childhood to life through journaling. Which ones would you write about?

Start with "What if?"

Related to picturing the impossible, but more grounded in reality, "what if" questions can take you to interesting places in your self-exploration. You can easily create "what if" questions by using conditional words such as *could, would, were,* and *was:*

>> What if I could . . .?

>> What if [object] did . . .?

>> What would happen if . . .?

But you can also take a more straightforward approach, such as "What if I owned a yacht?" or "What if I had five brothers?"

TIP

"What if" questions are fun to generate. But if you're drawing a blank or feel a bit lazy, open up a web browser and search for the phrase, *What if questions.* You can find more than enough questions to get you started.

When All Else Fails: Google *journaling prompts*

I put this tip last because it's the easiest and the most obvious way of getting new prompts. When you perform a web search for prompts, you get hundreds of thousands of results, each with ten or more different prompts. (When I googled it just now, I got 332,000 results.)

You can narrow the results down by adding a topic to your search. For example, *journaling prompts for gratitude* or "journaling prompts about love." The Internet is a great resource for unlimited journaling and writing prompts on any topic.

WARNING

One word of caution: Try not to go down a rabbit hole of online searching. Grab the first prompt that appeals to you and go with it. Keep in mind that you're searching because you want to enhance your journaling practice, not just gather a ton of prompts.

Index

O

obstacles, to journaling, 58–66
OneDrive, 46
organizing thoughts, 131–133
overcoming
fear, 58–66
obstacles to journaling, 58–66
resistance, 67–68
Oxford English Dictionary, 235

P

pages, indexing, 153–154
pain
expressing, 226–227
finding meaning in, 221–225
personifying, 230–232
releasing, 234–238
validating, 228–229
writing through, 225–234
patterns, journaling for, 27
pencils, 45
pens, 45
Penzu, 47
personifying pain, 230–232
"The person I am becoming is. . ." prompt, 128
perspective, renewing, 188–190
phrases, from books, as writing prompts, 395
physical health, 21–22
physical safety
as an advantage of digital journaling, 42
as a con of analog journaling, 40
plan of action
creating, 295–296
putting into action, 296–298
planning
future, 156
writing your plan, 70
positive affirmations, 162–163
Potter, Beatrix (writer), 13
practicing
bullet journaling over time, 147–154
creative journaling, 172–183
gratitude journaling, 200–203

uncommon gratitude, 203–209
preconceived notions, releasing your mind from, 158–160
preparing
for journaling, 31–50
journaling space, 48–50
to write, 122–123
present
focusing on awareness in the, 124–125
focusing on the (*see* mindful journaling)
importance of being, 109–110
"The present moment teaches me. . ." prompt, 128
Pressfield, Steven (author)
The War of Art, 67
priorities, identifying, 33–34
prioritizing
goals, 134–135
relationship with yourself, 354–358
privacy
as an advantage of digital journaling, 42
as a con of analog journaling, 40
processing mental inventory, 132–133
procrastination, avoiding, 67–68
productivity, for inspiration and achievement, 24
progress, reviewing, 297–298
props, 50
Psychosomatic Medicine: Journal of Biobehavioral Medicine, 21
purpose
establishing, 166–167
focusing on your, 78
staying true to your, 386

R

rational fear, 60
readjusting attitude, 191–192
recognizing
what you have, 196–197
your mindset, 287–290

recording events, 25–26
reducing stress levels, 187–188
reflect light, 75
reflecting
about, 232
on activities, 135–136
benefits of, 76–77
journaling for, 28
on the writing process, 127
on your feelings, 162
reflective journaling
about, 73
benefits of reflection, 76–77
deepening, 103–106
exploring life with, 73–77
focusing on purpose, 78
getting started with, 78–87
reflecting on writing process, 86–87
reflection overview, 75–76
setting time limits, 79
structuring your writing process, 80–86
writing through time, 87–103
relationships
about, 353–354
deepening friendships, 379–382
enhancing romantic partnerships, 367–373
evaluating with others, 360–366
finding empathy, 364–367
improving family relationships, 374–379
prioritizing with yourself, 354–358
releasing
inhibitions to self-expression, 160–163
pain, 234–238
playful side, 164–165
your mind from preconceived notions, 158–160
Remember icon, 3
reminders, setting, 55
renewing perspective, 188–190
resistance, overcoming, 67–68
responses, changing, 221–223

About the Author

Amber Lea Starfire is an author, editor, and creative-writing coach with a passion for journaling and helping others tell their life stories. An avid reader since the age of three, Amber began writing and keeping a simple diary at age eight. As a young adult, she discovered journaling and hasn't looked back. Since 2012, she has been blogging on the topics of journaling and memoir writing at http://writingthroughife.com.

Amber's previous books on journaling include *Journaling Through Relationships*, *Journaling the Chakras*, and *Week by Week: A Year's Worth of Journaling Prompts & Meditations*.

She is also the author of *Not the Mother I Remember: A Memoir* — finalist for the 2015 Next Generation Indie Book Awards and 2013–2014 Sarton Women's Literary Awards — and *Accidental Jesus Freak: One Woman's Journey from Fundamentalism to Freedom*, as well as co-editor of the award-winning anthology *Times They Were A-Changing: Women Remember the '60s & '70s*.

Amber lives with her partner Rich in the beautiful Napa Valley in California. In her spare time, Amber enjoys traveling by bicycle, gardening, and playing the piano.

Dedication

This book is dedicated to my mother, Jacquelyn B. Carr, PhD (1923–2007). An English teacher and writer herself, she opened my eyes to the world of books and of writing for personal development and expression. Thank you, Mom.

Author's Acknowledgments

I would like to thank Tracy Boggier for making this book possible and Project Manager Alissa Schwipps for your unending patience and reassurance as you walked me through the *For Dummies* author process.

To my writing critique group — Marilyn Campbell, Lenore Hirsch, Sarita Lopez, and Barbara Toboni — thank you for your patience and thoughtful feedback, and for trying a few of the many journaling prompts herein.

Thank you to my brother and sister-in-law, John and Vicki Carr, for hosting me and providing a stunning and peaceful place on the shores of Clear Lake, California to write the final chapters.

Thank you to my many clients, students, and readers who have shared your journal-writing journey with me over the years and helped me refine my methods.

And last but not least, thank you to my partner, Rich, for your limitless encouragement, patience, and support. I couldn't have done it without you.

Publisher's Acknowledgments

Senior Acquisitions Editor:
Tracy Boggier

Project Editor: Alissa Schwipps

Copy Editor: Laura Miller

Production Editor:
Magesh Elangovan

Cover Image: © Impact Photography/ Adobe Stock Photos